The Arcane Teaching

The Arcane Teaching

William Walker Atkinson

www.advancedthoughtpublishing.com

Published 2012 by Advanced Thought Publishing

The Arcane Teaching. Additional material copyright © 2012 by Advanced Thought Publishing. All rights reserved. ISBN: 978-0981318844

www.advancedthoughtpublishing.com

This book includes information from numerous sources. It is re-published for general reference and is not intended to be a substitute for independent verification by readers when necessary and appropriate. The book is sold with the understanding that neither the author nor publisher is engaged in rendering ay legal, medical or psychological advice. The publisher and author disclaim any personal liability, directly or indirectly, for advice or information presented within. Although the publisher and author have made every effort to ensure accuracy and completeness of the information, neither the publisher nor the author assumes any responsibility for errors, or for changes subsequent to publication. Further the publisher assumes no responsibility for author or third-party websites or their content.

Printed in the United States of America

10 9 8 7 6 5 4 3 2 1

Table of Contents

- **Part I. Fundamental Principles.**
  - Lesson I.The Arcane Teaching. 11
  - Lesson II.Absolute Law.. 19
  - Lesson III.Infinity of Nothingness 27

- **Part II. The Cosmos.**
  - Lesson IV.The Manifestation. 37
  - Lesson V.The Cosmic Will.. 45
  - Lesson VI.Involution And Evolution. 53

- **Part III. The Life of the Ego.**
  - Lesson VII.The One And The Many. 63
  - Lesson VIII.Metempsychosis. 71
  - Lesson IX.Survival of the Fittest....................................... 79

- **Part IV. Fate or Freedom?**
  - Lesson X.Fate and Destiny... 89
  - Lesson XI.Law, Order, and Sequence................................ 97
  - Lesson XII.Dominant Desire; Sovereign Will................. 105

- **Part V. The Astral Plane.**
  - Lesson XIII.Lower Astral Planes 115
  - Lesson XIV.Astral "Black-Keys.".. 123
  - Lesson XV.Higher Astral Planes....................................... 131

- **Part VI. Occult Forces.**
  - Lesson XVI.Psychic Phenomena. 141
  - Lesson XVII.Mentalism. 149
  - Lesson XVIII.Invocation and Evocation. 157

- **Part VII. Arcane Secrets.**
  - Lesson XIX.The Secret of the Opposites. 167
  - Lesson XX.The Secret of Rhythm. 175
  - Lesson XXI.The Secret of Balance..................................... 183

PART I. FUNDAMENTAL PRINCIPLES

Lesson I. The Arcane Teaching

Lesson II. Absolute Law

Lesson III. Infinity of Nothingness

The Arcane Teaching

LESSON I.
THE ARCANE TEACHING.

The Arcane Teaching has come down to the present age through the corridors of time, from the dim ages of past eras, races, and schools of thought. Even those highest in the councils of "The Custodians of The Scroll," are unable to trace the Teaching, in an unbroken direct line, further back than the time of Pythagoras (about 500 B. C), and a little later in Ancient Greece, although they find many references to, and extracts from, the teachings of ancient Egypt and Chaldea, which serve to show that the Pythagorean and Ancient Grecian Arcane Schools were founded on occult instruction still more remote, received in a direct line of succession of teachers and pupils extending over centuries. Investigators have found traces of the Arcane Teaching in the records of Persia and Medea, and it is believed that the inspiration for the original philosophical teaching (not the religion or the pessimism, however) of Gautama, the founder of Buddhism, was received from Arcane sources. Traces are also to be found in the Hebrew Esoteric Teachings of the "Kabballah" and the "Zohar."

The Grecian Arcane Teaching was undoubtedly obtained directly from Egyptian sources through Pythagoras, the relation between the early Grecian teaching and philosophies, and the older school of old Egypt, being very close and intimate. Pythagoras is known to have received instruction from Egyptian and Persian hierophants. Besides the traditions of the Arcanes, there is to be found the closest resemblance between the ancient Grecian teachings, and those of the Egyptian Esoteric Fraternities. Some of the Teachers, however, hold that the Grecian and Egyptian schools, respectively, were but two separate off-shoots of an original and older Teaching which had its origin in the lost continent of Atlantis. There are many Arcane traditions connecting the Teaching with Atlantis, and it is possible that both Egypt and Greece received it from this common source, instead of Greece being indebted to Egypt for the line of transmission. But, be this as it may, it is a fact that all of the traces of teaching that the various occult schools gather from the traditions, scraps of doctrine, and legends regarding Atlantis can be reconciled with the Grecian Arcane Teaching. And it is also a fact that the fragments of the Egyptian Esoteric Teachings, many of which are still preserved in an undoubted direct line of succession, are practically identical, in fundamental and basic points with the Grecian Arcane Teaching. And, as we have said, the Persian, Medean, and Chaldean legends and traditions, and scraps of teaching, show a common source of origin with that of ancient Greece.

We are speaking now of the historical view of the subject, alone. The traditions of the Arcanes hold that the Teaching, in some form, is as old as the race itself, and that it has been known to the advanced minds of every great civilization of the past, many of which disappeared thousands upon thousands of years ago, all traces of them having been lost to the present sub-race. The traditions hold that the Teaching was handed down from the Elder Brethren of the race—certain advanced souls who appeared in the earliest days, in order to plant the seeds of Truth, so that they would grow, blossom and bear fruit throughout the ages to follow. We do not ask you to accept this statement—it is not material—the Teaching bears the evidence of its own truth within itself, without needing the belief in any such authority. It agrees with the highest reason, and intuition of man, and to those who are ready to receive it, it shows itself as true. We mention the ancient traditions only that you may know what is accepted as truth by those high in authority among the Arcanes.

The word "Arcane" is derived from the Latin word, *"arcanus"* meaning "shut up, closed, hidden away," being derived from *"area"* meaning "a treasure chest." The English word means: "Hidden; concealed; secret; esoteric; mystic;" etc. So, the term "The Arcane Teaching," means "The Secret Doctrine."

The Arcanes are a loosely organized body of men, who have lived in all countries, in all times, since the days of the Ancient Greece, and probably for thousands of years before. They keep alive the old Teaching, traditions, legends, and instruction, and give the same to the few whom they meet who are deemed ready to receive the same. The *innermost* Teaching is never written or printed, and is passed from mouth to ear—from teacher to student—from hierophant to neophyte—as in the old days. Much of this inner Teaching is of a nature that renders it most advisable that it be reserved for the few, for it contains instruction of a nature that would cause it to be most dangerous were it to fall into unworthy hands. Even as it is, bits of it have leaked out, from time to time, and falling into the hands of unworthy persons have been used improperly. Every student of occultism is aware of the danger of which we speak. But the general principles of the Arcane Teachings have always been offered freely to those who felt attracted to them, and by them. Portions of them may be found in the various schools of the Hermetic Philosophy, and among the Roscrucian and similar teachings. In Freemasonry, there are hints of the ancient teachings, carefully disguised and unrecognized by the ordinary members of the order.

The exception to the rule regarding written or printed Teaching, is to be found in what the Arcanes know as "The Arcane Scroll," which contains many Arcane Aphorisms, or statements of Teaching, and which are written and renewed from time to time. The authorized copies are in the hands of special persons, high in the Arcane councils, who are known as "The Custodians of The Scroll," and who are to be found in every country of the globe, unknown and working silently. These persons belong to all walks of life, and society, and carefully avoid notoriety or public attention, in order to escape the sensational exploitation of the press, and the idle curiosity of the "wonder-seekers" who are to be found everywhere. While many of these Arcane Aphorisms have to do with the special branches of the Teachings, and are not allowed to be printed and distributed generally, still the Custodians have always been willing that the fundamental Aphorisms be quoted from in writings and books on the subject. Accordingly we shall embody a number of the Arcane Aphorisms in this series of lessons, always quoting them as such, and printing them in darker type, that they may be distinguished from our own comments and explanations and personal interpretations. These Aphorisms contain the highest occult truths, and principles, and we are very glad to have been accorded the privilege of presenting them to our students.

The Arcane Teaching is based upon the fundamental principle of the existence of an Absolute Supreme Power, which is the Cause and Reason of the Cosmos and all the manifestations contained therein—all that men call "the universe." This Absolute Supreme Power is known in the Arcane Teaching as "THE LAW," and is represented in the symbols by the word "Lex."

The Law is regarded as an Abstract Principle of Power, impossible of being represented by words or even by symbols. It is not a Pantheistic Deity, or Being—It is an Absolute *Principle,* beyond definition or description. It does not manifest Itself in a universe of shapes and forms, by separating Itself into the Many as the Pantheistic Being is held to do in certain philosophies. Instead of this It *causes* Universal Being to proceed from Infinite Not-Being—*causes* the Cosmos to arise from Chaos—*causes* Manifestation to arise from the Unmanifest—*causes* Everything to arise from Infinite Nothing. The Law is not Being—but the Cause of Being. It cannot be said to "Be," in the ordinary sense—It *causes* the verb "To Be" to have a meaning.

The Arcane Teaching is not Pantheism, either expressed or implied—either frankly stated, or subtly concealed behind words. The Absolute can never become the Relative. The Law can never separate Itself into bits of "You and I." Nor is the Cosmos to be regarded as a nightmare dream; meditation; illusion; delusion; or imagination; of the Absolute, as some of the philosophical schools of India, and the pessimistic schools of the West, would have men believe, against all the natural intuition of the race. The Law does not dream, meditate, imagine, or "think"—neither is it deluded, or subject to illusion, delusion or "ignorance," as some have taught. These are but qualities belonging to *beings*—the Law is above beings, and even above Being. To hold otherwise is to degrade It, and to deny Its Absoluteness.

The Arcane Teaching holds that other than The Law there is but Infinity, which is Nothingness. The Teaching distinguishes between the Absolute Law and Infinity, in which it differs from the majority of other philosophies which holds them to be identical. But this daring conception is defended and proven to be logical by the Arcane Teachers, and in this teaching is to be found the only rational explanation of the Cause and Manifestation of the Cosmos. The Nothingness of Infinity, is not a condition of "Not-ness," but a condition or state of "NoThingness." Infinity is an Infinite No-Thing, in which, however, sleeps the latency, possibility, potency, and promise, of Everything, past, present, and future. In its Infinite Nothingness, *no thing* IS in actuality, but *every thing* is in latency and possibility, under The Law. The Arcane Teaching on the subject of the Infinity of Nothingness, is a startling revelation to those who have been searching for the Truth in other philosophies, but who have found themselves wandering 'round and 'round in a mental circle—never arriving anywhere. The Infinity of Nothingness is capable of logical and rational proof. This doctrine flies squarely in the face of the current philosophical dogmas of "From Nothing, no thing comes," or "Ex Nihilo, nihil fit." On the contrary it boldly asserts "From Nothing, Everything comes," or "Ex Nihilo, Omnis fit." But it must be remembered, that this Nothing contains within itself the Possibility, latency, and promise of Everything. It is a No-Thing, instead of a "Not."

The Arcane Teachings hold that at the expiration of the great cycle of time—after aeons of Cosmic Night, or Period of Infinite Nothingness, The Law moves over the emptiness of Infinity, and the first activities of a new Cosmic Day, or Manifest Cosmos, begin to show themselves. The first manifestation is the Cosmic Will, or Life Principle.

This Cosmic Will is the One Life of the Cosmos, which many philosophies mistakenly claim to be the Absolute Itself. It is the Universal Being, but it is under The Law, and relative to It, and is not absolute. From this Cosmic Will, Logos, Demiurge, World-Spirit, or Universal Life Principle, is manifested, the Cosmos or Manifested Universe of life, shape and form. The Cosmos is *alive* in every part, and its real nature vests in the Cosmic Will, which is ever behind, under, and in, all manifestations of the universal activities, from lowest to highest. Here is the World Spirit, or Pantheistic One-All—*but it is under The Law!*

In the Cosmos is contained "The Three Principles"—of Substance, Motion, and Consciousness; respectively. From the Three Principles arise all the infinite variety of combinations of mind, energy and matter, which go to make up the varieties of manifestation in the universe. The Arcane Teaching includes the doctrine of Perpetual Evolution of Substance, Energy, and Consciousness, respectively, on all the various planes of activity. The Teaching is that there are infinite planes of evolution, in groups of seven, which are sub-divided in seven, and so on.

The Arcane Teaching holds that the Cosmos is regulated by "The Seven Laws," which are superimposed by The Law upon the Cosmic Will, and thus upon all that is manifested. These Seven Cosmic Laws are as follows:

I. *The Law of Orderly Trend.* Under this law there is always manifested law and order in the Cosmos, from suns to atoms; from highest to lowest; matter, energy, and mind. There is no Disorder, Inharmony, or Chance in the Cosmos.

II. *The Law of Analogy.* Under this law, there is found a correspondence and agreement between all of the various forms of manifestation. What is true of the atom, is true of the sun. What is true of the amoeba is true of man, and beings above man. What is true of matter, is true of energy and mind. To know one is to know all. "As above, so below," as the Hermetists express it. *"Ex Uno disce Omnes"*—"From One know All," as the Arcane axiom says. This law is applied in studying the higher planes—they may be known by the lower, just as solar systems may be known by studying the atoms and molecules.

III. *The Law of Sequence.* Under this Law, there is included the activities of what is generally known as "Cause and Effect." Nothing happens by chance. Nothing happens without a precedent manifestation, and a subsequent manifestation. Everything has its "before and after" things. Nothing stands alone, and independent of what has gone before, nor can it escape from acting upon that which comes after. Everything proceeds from something, and is succeeded by something.

IV. *The Law of Rhythm.* Under this law falls a variety of phenomena, among which is the important phenomenon of Vibration. Everything is in constant vibration—everything material, mental or of *energy.* Upon this fact depends the variety, degrees, states and conditions of the manifestations of the Cosmos. All is in vibration—physical, mental and spiritual. Vibration is the key of relative power, and relative activities. To control Vibration is to control all forces in the universe. The control of Vibrations forms an important part of the Arcane formulas.

V. *The Law of Balance.* Under this law there is to be found an explanation for the universal equilibrium, compensation and balance, observed in all of the manifestations of the Cosmos. One thing balances another, in the physical, mental and spiritual. Everything has something set opposite it, to balance it. Everything has its compensation. Everything has its Cosmic price. In an understanding of the Law of Balance, there is to be found the Secret of Power and Poise. The Arcane Teaching contain formulas for Balance.

VI. *The Law of Cyclicity.* Under this law is found the cyclic, or circular trend of all things, physical, mental and spiritual. Everything moves in circles. The wise and strong convert the circles into spirals. Instead of traveling around in an eternal circle, the wise and strong rise in spirals to attainment and advancement. Worlds and atoms; Cosmos and Man; all are under this law, and move in accordance therewith. To convert the Circle into the Spiral, is one of the Arcane Secrets, conveyed in its formulas.

VII. *The Law of Opposites,* Under this law is to be found the explanation of that wonderful fact in nature—the fact that everything has its opposite; everything *is,* and *is not,* at the same time; everything has its other side; every truth is but a half-truth; everything is a paradox; every thesis has its anti-thesis; every truth contains a bit of untruth, and every untruth a bit of truth; every male contains female—every female contains male. Also the fact that opposite things are alike, in the end; that extremes meet; the contradictions may be reconciled. In this great Cosmic law is found the fact that diametrically opposite things, physical, mental and spiritual, are in reality but the different poles of the same thing. In this law is found the Mystery of Polarity—in it vests the Secret of Sex—Generation and Regeneration—the Arcane Teaching embraces all these.

The Arcane Teaching, as presented in these Lessons, will include the Arcane Formulas whereby the Seven Laws may be applied under the mind and will of the individual, enabling him to take advantage of the flood-tide of Rhythm, and to neutralize the ebb-tide; to enable him to neutralize the Opposites; to find and hold the Balance and Poise; to convert the Cycles into Rising Spirals; to take advantage of the Law of Sequence—thus to Master Fate, instead of being her Slave; to conquer laws by laws; to oppose principle to principle; to acquire the Art of Mental Alchemy, or Transmutation of Mental States and Conditions. These and many other fields of occult knowledge will the Arcane Teaching open out to the earnest seeker. To those who are ready, this Teaching will appeal. Do you feel attracted to it—then follow the leading of your intuition. If not, pass it by for the present, for you are not prepared—instead call the attention of some person more ready, to it, and thus be an instrument of The Law.

The Arcane Teaching

LESSON II.
ABSOLUTE LAW.

The Arcane Scroll contains the following Aphorisms regarding this Supreme Power, which in the Arcane Teaching is known as "THE LAW."

APHORISM I. "The Law IS."

APHORISM II. "Beyond The Law there IS Not. Higher than The Law there IS Not. Elder than the Law there IS Not."

APHORISM III. "The Law is the Absolute. Existing beyond Time, and Space, and Change; transcending the Three Principles and the Seven Laws; It ever hath been, ever is, and ever shall be. Ever Unique; Unconditioned; Immutable; Self-Existent; Self-Sufficient; Independent; Abstract; It dwelleth Unknowable, Unthinkable, Ineffable."

APHORISM IV. "The Law is the Efficient Reason of All-Things; and is the Supreme Power and Causer."

A consideration of the above four Aphorisms will throw light on the inner meanings contained within them. Let us now consider them in detail:

APHORISM I. "The Law Is." In this Aphorism the word "IS" denotes "present, actual existence." It is as strong a term denoting actual existence as the English language supplies. But, in the ancient Arcane terminology its Grecian equivalent was used in a still stronger sense than the ordinary use of the word "is" indicates. In the English language, the word "is" is used as the third person singular of the verb "Be," in the indicative mood, present tense. But the words "is" and "be" have two entirely different original meanings, particularly when considered from the point of view of the ancient Arcane schools. To explain further: The Word "Be" is derived from the Greek word "phuo," meaning: "to bring forth; to produce; to be born;" etc., the original meaning signifying beginning in time; existence of a preceding cause; relativity, etc. And, accordingly, the ancient Greek philosophers, especially those of the Arcane schools, used the term "be" and "being" to denote the relative existence of the phenomenal or manifested universe, and not in the sense of absolute existence. The word "is," on the contrary, is desired from the word, "esti" which in turn was derived from the Sanscrit word "asti" both of which denote "existence," in its absolute sense, without reference to birth, bringing forth, or production. In its true and Arcane significance the word "is" is analogous to "am," which had its origin in the Sanscrit "as" signifying absolute existence, which significance was also imparted to analogous words in the Hebrew, Egyptian and other Oriental languages. The word "is" has the significance of the word "Am" in the following quotation from Exodus, iii. 14, in the Hebrew Sacred Books: "And God said unto Moses, 'I AM That I AM'; and he said, Thus shalt thou say unto the children of Israel: I AM hath sent me unto you." This then is the sense in which the Arcane Aphorism employs the term "IS"—in the sense of Absolute Existence. We have taken the pains to explain this to you at length, not for the purpose of verbal hair-splitting, but in order to bring out the true occult meaning of the term. This, particularly, because we shall use the term "Being" in its relative sense in connection with the Cosmos, as we proceed. Remember that there is no "IS-ness" other than that of The Law—all other "is-ness" is but "Being" which is relative, created, and phenomenal. In the true sense, there is no IS other than the existence of The Law. For this reason we shall always print the word in capital letters when we use it in its Arcane significance.

Aphorism II. "Beyond The Law there IS Not. Higher than The Law there IS Not. Elder than The Law there IS Not." In these three sentences is taught the Absolute Omnipresence; the Absolute Supremacy; the Eternity; and the Self-Existence of The Law. There is naught beyond It, for there is no beyond; there is naught elder than It, for it is eternal and self-existent, there being nothing precedent to It to have caused or created It. We must here ask you to consider the fact that the Aphorism uses the term "Not," instead of "Nothing," for the reason that the Arcane meaning of the two terms is different. In the Arcane sense, the word "Not" means absolute negation—that is it denotes the absence of "is-ness," or "am-ness," and also the absence of even relative "being." "Not" means absolute not-ness— a condition of non-existence past, present, or future; absolute or relative. It is a positive denial of any existence whatsoever, of any kind, character, or degree, past, present or future. Further than this, language cannot go. But the words: "Nothing," and "Nothingness," although generally used as meaning "not-ness" in the sense just mentioned, have an entirely different Arcane significance and meaning. In the Aphorisms, and in all of the Arcane Teaching these words are used in a relative sense, a capital "N" being employed to denote the said use of the word. We shall consider this "Nothingness," a little later on.

APHORISM III. The first sentence is: "The Law is Absolute." In this sentence is stated the highest truth capable of being expressed in words. Let us examine the term and see what it really means. "Absolute" means, in its original and essential significance: "Unbound; Free; Unfettered; Unrestrained." There are a number of derivative meanings, but the above definition gives the essential meaning of the term—and that meaning may be reduced to one word: "FREE." In other words, Absoluteness means Perfect Freedom—Sovereignty—Supremacy. There can be nothing higher than Absoluteness. There can be nothing over Absoluteness. There can be no Power beyond Absoluteness. The "Law" of a thing, or things, is the sovereign power that exercises a control over it And an Absolute Law is the supreme, highest and unqualified Power over all things. Therefore is the Absolute called Law—therefore is The Law called Absolute. The term, Absolute Law is the highest and most positive term in the language, expressing Power and Control. There can be nothing that can oppose such Power; or run contrary to It, or overrule It, or "break" It. It is Power Absolutely Supreme.

The Absolute Law must not only be Self-Governed and Uncontrolled, but must also be Self-Existent and Causeless, for if there were aught else to have created It, or to have caused It to exist, then that "other" would be the Absolute. The very meaning of the term precludes any outside Cause affecting It—It is Causeless; and It exists of, and because of, Itself. To speak of aught causing, governing, or binding the Absolute, is to utter words that have no meaning. And even if we postulate a Supreme Being, governed by the "laws of His own inner nature," then these "inner laws," rather than the Supreme Being are the Absolute. So, you see that at the last the Law and the Absolute must be the one and the same.

The Aphorism continues: Existing beyond, Time, and Space and Change transcending the Three Principles and the Seven Laws; It hath ever been, ever is, and ever shall be. The words: "Is, hath, ever been, and ever shall be," denotes the Eternality of The Law," for a Self-Existent, Causeless, Absolute, must be Eternal—for naught could have caused it, nor could aught ever terminate it. "Beyond Time and Space" expresses Its Omnipresence and Eternality—Time and Space belong to the Infinite

Nothingness, which is subject to the Absolute Law. "Transcending the Three Principles and the Seven Laws"—by this is meant the Three Principles of the Cosmos, and the Seven Laws by which The Law manifests Itself through the Cosmos, when the latter emerges in Manifestation from the Unmanifest, Infinity of Nothingness. "Transcending", means, of course: "surpassing; surmounting; being above"; "being beyond"; etc. As the Three Principles are aspects of the Cosmos; and the Seven Laws are caused by The Absolute Law, it follows that the latter is superior and over them. "Ever Unique; Unconditioned; Immutable; Self-Existent; Self-Sufficient; Independent; and Abstract"—let us consider the meaning of each of the words composing this remarkable sentence:

Ever: "Always; forever; continually; without cessation."

Unique: "Without a like or equal; unmatched; Unparalleled; sole."

Unconditioned: "Not subject to conditions or limitations; hence, inconceivable; incognitable."

Immutable: "Unchangeable; invariable; changeless."

Self-Existent: "Free from Cause; existing independent of aught else."

Self-Sufficient: "Sufficient for self, without aid or co-operation."

Independent: "Not dependent; not subject to control; not relying on aught; not subordinate or coordinate."

Abstract: "Apart from aught else; separate from aught else; existing apart and in Itself"; etc.

The above definitions need no further explanation or comment—they tell their own tale, and convey the meaning of the Aphorism clearly, when thus defined. The Aphorism closes with the following words: "It dwelleth Unknowable; Unthinkable; Ineffable." These three words have the following meaning:

Unknowable: "That which cannot be known, being too difficult or subtle for the human intellect"; etc.

Unthinkable: "That which cannot be made an object of thought; incapable of being thought; incognitable; eluding the understanding"; etc.

Ineffable: "Incapable of being expressed in words; inexpressible; indescribable"; etc.

The combined idea of the three terms is well expressed by Herbert Spencer in his famous sentence; "By continually seeking to know, and being continually thrown back with a deepened conviction of the impossibility of knowing, we may keep alive the consciousness that it is alike our highest wisdom and our highest duty to regard that through which all things exist as The Unknowable." Or, as Edwin Arnold in his "Light of Asia" voices the beginning of the teachings of the Buddha:

> "Om, Amitaya! measure not with words
> Th' Immeasurable: nor sink the string of thought
> Into the Fathomless, who asks doth err,
> Who answers, errs. Say naught!
> Shall any gazer see with mortal eyes;
> Or any searcher know with mortal mind?
> Veil after veil will lift—but there must be
> Veil upon veil behind."

But, it may be asked: If The Law is Unknowable, Unthinkable, and Ineffable, then why do you attempt to inform us regarding It; why do you attempt to teach us about It? The answer, O Neophyte, is this: We seek not to explain the unexplainable Law to you—we strive not to describe its nature to you, for that would be impossible, there being no words to express It, and no minds capable of understanding It were It explained. The Aphorism expresses this truth fully and emphatically. But we do desire to impress upon your minds and understanding, the fact that It IS. Not only do we ask you to believe this because the Arcane Teaching is the repository of the reports of the highest minds of the race—the illumined of all ages—but also because the intellect and intuition of every advanced man reports to him this truth, and informs him that back of, beyond, over and under, and in All, there is the Supreme Law.

No matter what may be his religion, ancient or modern; or his lack of religion—no matter what may be his philosophy, metaphysics or theology, named or unnamed—no matter upon what lines he may have thought, if he has thought at all—Man must ever recognize the report of his reason, and his intuition, which informs him of the existence of a Supreme and Universal Law, governing all things. To deny this, is to deny reason. Faith is not required—reason suffices and fully informs that The Law IS. And with that IS-ness, the report ceases—the knowledge is then known, to low and high alike. While advanced beings on higher planes have reported great knowledge regarding the Cosmos, they state positively that they know no more regarding the nature of The Law than does the humble thinker on our own plane. But from the highest comes the same report as that which informs the mind of the lowest—The Law IS. Therefore in asking you to accept this report of the illumined, the highest of the race, including those whom we call the Elder Brethren, we ask you to accept only that which your own reason informs you to be a basic truth—The Law IS.

It is true that the race has built around the conception of the Absolute Law, the varying conceptions of personal deities, and pantheistic beings, but analyze them all and you will find that the reason for the activities of these deities, personal or pantheistic, has been the desire; will; want; inclination or "inner-laws" which are supposed to actuate their manifestations, or incite their activities, either consciously, unconsciously; or according to some of the Hindu schools, because of ignorance, illusion, or self-deception. In short, all of these conceptions of deity are Beings who are actuated by motives, feelings, desires of "inner-laws," just as are men, and other manifested or created things. The anthropomorphic idea is evidenced not only in the crude conceptions of deity held by the savages, but also in the higher concepts; and even in the conceptions of a Pantheistic Being, or Absolute Being held by some of the philosophers and religious teachers of East and West. The pantheistic conception is utterly illogical, for as Schopenhauer says: "When we think of Nature as God, we show God to the door." And as the Arcane Teachers point out, even admitting any of these conceptions of Being, the mind must see that in the "inner law" that moves Being to activity—the Law of Itself—there alone is to be found the Absolute. In such case the Law not the Being, is the Absolute, for it is the causer, and controller, and mover, and reason of the universe.

It is true that some of the philosophers and teachers try to explain away this fact, by saying that "Being and Law" are One. But this is no solution, for even if that be admitted, then the Law within the Being is the Efficient Reason and Causer of Action, and the rest of the Being is controlled, acted upon and moved by the Law within it. The whole idea of Being must be discarded in considering the Absolute. The Absolute is, and can be, only Law. For in all conceptions, The LAW is, and must be, seen to be the Ultimate Cause of all activity. The advocates of Absolute Being, object that they are unable to conceive of Law without a Lawgiving Being. But, considering this answer, we soon see that in order for the Lawgiving Being to proceed to give or promulgate Law, it must be moved by some inner law, desire, want, or will of its own nature—and that simply pushes back the question one step further. Try as we may, we cannot escape the conviction that LAW is the First, and Last Cause—the Beginning and the Ending—the Efficient Reason of All-Things. Law is not a Being—not a Mind—not a Spirit—not a Thing—It is LAW, and naught else. We must accept It as Absolute Power, and as the Aphorisms present It to us. Beyond this we cannot go. Examine the Aphorisms carefully, and you will find that they agree fully with the highest reports of your reason, and in no way run contrary to it.

Aphorism IV. The Law is the Efficient Reason of All-Things, and is the Supreme Power and Causer of the Cosmos.

In this Aphorism is stated plainly and clearly the truth that The Law is the Supreme Power of the Cosmos, and the Causer thereof. The term "Efficient Reason" conveys the entire truth regarding the creation of or evolution of the Cosmos. Let us consider the definition of the two words composing the term, in order to see the meaning still more clearly:

Efficient: "Causing or producing effects or results; acting as the cause of effects; a prime mover; actively operative; etc."

Reason: "An efficient cause; a final cause; explanation; that which explains or accounts for anything; motive of action; etc."

The Cosmos is explainable only by The Law. Without The Law there could be no Cosmos. The Law is the cause of the Cosmos, and of every manifestation within it. The very word "Cosmos" is derived from the Greek word meaning: "the universe as governed by law." Not only the Arcane Teaching, but modern science states as its first axiom: "The Cosmos is Governed by Law." To those who prefer the idea of an anthropomorphic Being, or a World-Spirit, as the Absolute, we have to say that, unfortunately for their idea, the facts of the Cosmos are all against them—Law is everywhere seen to be dominant and sovereign, even in its relative manifestations. We cannot escape it, and should not desire to; and will not desire to, when we understand its meaning. The explanation of this must wait until its proper place in these lessons is reached. Enough for the present to state that in all human ideas of Law there is to be found the correlated ideas of Justice and Equity. Know then that this relative idea, when transformed to the absolute plane, results in the identification of Absolute Justice and Absolute Equity, with the Absolute Law. Could mortal ask more? Has he aught to fear of Absolute Equity and

Justice? Can he not postulate in the Absolute all the highest conceptions of Fair Play that he finds in himself? The Cosmos is Governed by Law!

LESSON III.
INFINITY OF NOTHINGNESS.

We now invite you to consider the correlative principle of Truth, in which is set forth the Infinity of Nothingness—Chaos—the Unmanifest; from which, *under The Law,* emerges Everything—the Cosmos—the Manifest. We have informed you that The Law is not a Pantheistic Being, either breaking Itself into bits, or parts, in order to create Universes; neither does It imagine, mentally create, dream, or meditate into existence a false and fictitious Universe "all in its mind," as pseudo-occultism and pessimistic philosophies would have you believe. Listen to the Aphorism:

Aphorism V. "Other than The Law, there is but Infinity, which is Nothingness. But in that Infinity of Nothingness, there is Unmanifest, the Latency, Possibility, Futurity, Potentiality, and Promise of Manifest Everythingness. It is *the* Chaos from which, under The Law, emerges the Cosmos, It is the Womb of the Cosmos."

Postponing for the moment the consideration of the distinction between the Absolute and Infinity, which is uncommon in ordinary modern thought, we wish to call your attention to the fact that Infinity is not designated as "Not," or as partaking of "notness," but is spoken of as "Nothingness," which is a state of Nothing. In the Arcane Teaching the words: "Nothing" and "Nothingness," signify "No-Thing," and "No-Thingness," respectively. This may seem like metaphysical hair-splitting, but it is not. Not having common words to express uncommon ideas, philosophers must needs split common words into shades of meaning and significance, or else remain silent with their thoughts unexpressed. In order to understand "No-Thingness," and a "No-Thing," you must understand the meaning of the word "Thing" to which these words are opposed. A "Thing" is "whatever exists as a separate object of sense or thought," in the sense of *being* and having apparent qualities which can be thought of in terms of sense-perception, such as size, shape, form, etc.—something connected directly or indirectly with physical appearance—something of the relative universe—something having a correspondence in experience. And Nothingness must be the opposite of Thingness.

Therefore the Aphorism practically says that Infinity is a "Latency" that is No-Thing in reality, but yet has an existence of some kind, at least potentially. It can contain naught actually apparent to the senses; naught that can be experienced; naught that can be sensed; naught that can be thought of by the intellect, nor pictured in the imagination—in short, nothing that is capable of inducing a mental image in your mind. And yet it *exists* (if the word can be used) as a state or condition in which all is in Latency, Possibility, Futurity, Potentiality, and Promise. In short, it is The Unmanifest containing All Manifestation within it in latency, possibility and futurity, awaiting the force of The Law to bid it conceive, produce, and bring forth Being. We shall learn about this Infinite Nothingness shortly, in connection with another Aphorism. Enough for the present to realize the words of the Aphorism before us, which informs us that other than The Law there is Not, with the exception of the Infinity of Nothingness which exists in latency. Other than The Law, there IS Not in the absolute sense.

Philosophies and schools of metaphysics have generally confused the meaning of the two terms "absolute" and "relative," and have used them as identical in meaning. The Arcane Teaching makes a sharp distinction between the two terms, however—not a difference based upon a metaphysical hair-splitting tendency, but because there are two entirely different ideas which must be expressed in these two words, and, in spite of the customs of the metaphysicians the distinction must be made. We do not wish to lead you into an extended metaphysical discussion, but we think that you should be taught to make this important distinction in the true meaning of these terms.

The term "absolute," in its true sense and essential meaning, implies an *apartness; separation; independence; self-existence; self-sufficiency; supreme; unfettered; free.* The "essence of the essence" of its meaning is to be found in the words "free, independent, self-sufficient." And when used in connection with the word "law," it represents the Supreme Power, depending upon no other power; its own sovereign; and the ruler of all else, without restriction. This conception we have in The Absolute Law, which is the Independent, Free, Sovereign Lord of All.

The term "infinite" has an entirely different meaning, in its true sense, although the philosophers and metaphysicians often add to it the attributes of the Absolute, which is a mistake. The word "infinite" in its true sense and essential meaning, implies *a state of boundlessness; limitlessness; not circumscribed; as to time, space, variety, possibilities, combination, shape, form, etc.* Its essence may be understood by referring to the words from which it sprung, i.e., the Latin words *"in"* meaning *"not"*; and *"finitus"* meaning *"finished"* In short, the word "infinite" means *"not finished; not complete; capable of unlimited manifestation, and possibilities"* So, you see, while the idea of "Absolute" means *fixed, complete independent* state or condition; "Infinite" means a state of endless and unlimited possibilities of manifestation and expression.

The true philosophical idea of Infinity, consists of the conception of any sort of mental object as having the quality of quantity which cannot be exhausted by any succession of experiences, however prolonged or extended, in time, space, variety, or number. By holding this idea in mind, you will never make the mistake of confounding infinity with absoluteness, hereafter. The chief cause of the confusion arises from the unauthorized use of the term "infinite" in relation to "power." *Power belongs to the Absolute, and is not one of the attributes of Infinity.* "Infinite Power" would mean an infinite possibility of the *manifestation* and *expression* of unlimited power; while Absolute Power means *all the Power there is,* fixed, independent and sovereign, unvarying and immutable, and not subject to changes of degree, etc. Absolute Law is *not* an infinite capacity for expression of power—It is *Power-in-Itself.*

All the great thinkers of all times, esoteric and exoteric, have agreed in this idea of the Infinite being the Unlimited Possibility. The best of the ancient Greek philosophers, from Aristotle down, held to this idea. As Schopenhauer says: "It is already a doctrine of Aristotle, that Infinity can never be *actu* (actual, given, fixed) but only *potentia* (in possibility, latency, promise, potentiality)." And as Lewes says: "If Zero is the sign of a vanished quantity, the Infinite is the sign of continuity." We trust that you now see that the Absolute could never become Relative or Many—and that the Infinite alone is capable of endless changes in shape, form, variety, in time, space, and number; and contains within itself the *promise, possibility, latency, and potentiality of Everything.*

The Arcane Teachers, in the olden time, illustrated this to their pupils by the following symbols: The figure "1" standing for the Absolute, and being fixed, independent, sovereign, and alone. By itself, and in itself it is incapable of multiplying or dividing—multiply anything by "1"; or divide anything by "1," and the thing remains unchanged. Multiply or divide "1" by itself, and the answer still is "1," showing that the Absolute cannot be increased or divided, even by itself. Subtract "1" from itself, and the result is "0," showing that if the Absolute were subtracted from it would cease to exist, and there would be naught left but the Infinite Nothingness. Then the Teachers called the attention of the pupil to the Zero, or "Infinite Nothing" symbol, i.e., "0." In itself, "0" means Nothing. Multiply or divide anything by "0," and the answer is always "0." Multiply "0" by itself, and "0" remains—the Infinite cannot increase itself, for in its circle it includes All Possibility. But divide "0" by itself—and lo! "0 into 0 goes 1 time": the answer is "1," showing that if the Infinite be divided by itself, the Absolute is found to be at its centre, undisturbed, independent, self-existent. The symbol of Infinity, in mathematics, however, is not "0" or Unmanifest Infinity, but ∞ which indicates Manifest Infinity, the symbol always indicating endless continuation of action.

Now the symbol of the Infinite Nothing, becoming Infinite Everything. Place a string of "O's," as follows: 000,000,000,000,000—you see that they still mean "Nothing." Now place "1" (the symbol of the Absolute), before the string and we have 1,000,000,000,000,000, which we may enlarge to infinite number by the addition of "O's." Or place the Absolute "1," behind the string, and we have .000,000,000,000,000,1, a very small decimal, which may be carried to infinitesimal smallness by the addition of "O's." Thus we see, by symbols, that the action of the Absolute Law on the Infinite Nothingness produces Infinite Greatness, or Infinite Smallness.

Now that you understand that Infinity means the Infinite *Possibility* of Things, rather than an Infinite Manifest *Thing,* you may be able to see that the Infinity of Nothingness of the Arcane Teaching is not quite so irrational as it appeared at first sight. In order to realize the truth of the Aphorism still more forcibly, let us consider what Infinity (even in the ordinary use of the term) really is. You will find that all thought if analyzed, implies the Nothingness of Infinity.

Non-Being, or Nothingness, was always regarded by certain schools of the ancient Greek philosophy, as existent in a philosophical sense. Empty space was considered as truly existent as the atoms which afterward appeared in space. Plato regarded Empty Space as the matrix, or mould, in which the universe was formed. He held that there was possible an abstract realization of pure empty space, which is Nothing; the Void, which is the all-containing receptacle of creative energy, and in which being, first distinguished into geometrical figures, becomes the framework of the physical world. Scotus held that since Deity creates the world out of Nothing, then Nothing must exist as an emanation of Deity. Hegel distinguished between a *"nicht"* or "Not" ;. and a *"nichts"* or "Nothing." Theology has always held that Deity "created the universe from Nothing," thereby implying at least a quasi-existence of Infinite Nothingness. Spinoza recognized an "infinitely infinite" which is practically an Infinite Nothing. Plato said that "Space as a Thing is incredible, difficult of explanation, most difficult to comprehend." And Zeno, the Eleatic, said: "If Space is a Thing, it must be *in* Something, and so in Space; for everything that is, is *in* Something, and so in Space; and so on *ad infinitum*. Therefore, Space is *not* a Thing." So much for the philosophers. Let us see what our own reason informs us.

Let us first examine the idea of Space. Space is the mental symbol for Infinity. Consider yourself as standing at a fixed point in Space—then you must realize that there exists an infinite distance or extension in Space, from that point, in an infinite number of directions. Leaving out of consideration all objects in space—considering Pure Empty Space—and you must see that there is an *endless extension* possible, in innumerable directions—extension without end. Imagine a number of miles represented in *a row of figures extending from earth to the most distant star;* then multiply that number by itself; and then the product by itself; and so on, for a time equal to the number of years since the Cosmic Day began. Then you would have a number of miles, the written figures of which would fill all the space that your mind is able of even conceiving. Then think of a Being traveling to the extent of that measurement—would he then be near the end of space? No! the distance traveled by him would be as a mathematical "Nothing" or Zero, compared with Infinite Space. No mathematician could have figured out the infinitesimal smallness of the fraction denoting the comparison, were he to have worked continually since the dawn of the Cosmic day. The calculation would be endless, because the result would be infinitesimal, and at the end, he would have to place the sign of "infinity" back of it. Just think! *To be able to travel for all Eternity through Space without coming to an end!* You cannot come to an end of Space, even in thought or imagination—try it! You will find that think as *far* as you will into Space, there must always be Infinite Space *beyond* that imagined point. There is "no up or down" in Space. Space is something with its centre *everywhere,* and its circumference *nowhere.* At the last, philosophy and science are compelled to hold that "Space is merely the *possibility* of infinite extension; or the *infinite possibility* of extension"—to the Universal Ether. In the end, Ether is called the Great Mystery of Science. It must be considered as a Nothing that is a Something. A leading scientific lecturer said, and wrote, recently: "The Ether is unconditioned, an entity of *no properties but of all possibilities,* or, more exactly, not an entity at all, but *an infinite possibility."* And, so we find, even Matter and Things themselves, arising from and being resolved into an Infinite Nothingness that is also Infinite Possibility.

Now, for a moment, let us endeavor to imagine the condition or state of the Infinity of Nothingness—the Unmanifest Cosmos—during the Cosmic Night, and before the faintest dawn of the new Cosmic Day. The Three Cosmic Principles are resolved into the condition of the Unmanifest, but are not destroyed—there are Nothing, but *not* "Not!" The Three Cosmic Principles are Substance; Motion; and Consciousness, respectively. Substance has assumed its most subtle form, infinitely rarer and finer than the finest ether—it is practically Nothing, but yet exists in latency, possibility, and promise. Motion has assumed a rate of vibration so high that it is practically at Rest, although not destroyed—it is still Motion in latency. Consciousness has assumed the condition of a deep unconsciousness—a profound dreamless sleep; a swoon following upon the infinite ecstasy of the Supreme Cosmic Consciousness of the previous Cosmic Day. It knows Nothing; is conscious of Nothing—for there is but Nothing of which it could be conscious, or could know, for all manifestation has ceased until the dawn of the new Cosmic Day. It is even unconscious of the presence and power of The Law, although The Law still reigns over it, and will awaken it once more, as it has many times before, in the Eternal Chain of Cosmic Days and Nights.

The Cosmos sleeps in the condition of Infinite Nothingness—the Unmanifest! The Abyssmal Abyss—the Eternal Deep—the Face of the Waters—the Void—the Cosmic Womb! The Mother Sleeps! The Laws of Cyclic Rhythm have brought to Her the Rest of the Cosmic Night! But she will awaken and greet her Supreme Lord at the dawn of the Cosmic Day. From the Cosmic Womb will proceed The Cosmic Will, which will manifest the universe of universes; infinitudes of infinitudes of shape, form, and variety, of things, life, and beings. In her Existence is the Promise of all that Shall Be throughout the Ages and Aeons of Eternities of Eternities. The Mother sleeps, sleeps, sleeps! But, through the Night, as through the Day, THE LAW IS, immutable, unchanged, Absolute.

PART II. THE COSMOS.

Lesson IV. The Manifestation.
Lesson V. The Cosmic Will.
Lesson VI. Involution and Evolution.

The Arcane Teaching

LESSON IV.
THE MANIFESTATION.

This is the Arcane Teaching regarding the process whereby the Unmanifest becomes Manifest; the Latency becomes Activity; the Possibility becomes Actuality; the Potentiality becomes Reality; the Promise becomes Fulfilment. Listen to the Aphorism:

Aphorism VI. "During the aeons of the Cosmic Night, The Law dwells Alone, in solitude; The Cosmos remains resolved into its condition of the Unmanifest—the Infinity of Nothingness. Then comes the dawn, when The Law superimposes the Infinity of Nothingness, and causes the Unmanifest to become Manifest; the Nothing to become Everything; Latency to become Activity; Potentiality to become Reality; Promise to become Fulfillment."

At the extreme swing of the pendulum of Rhythm—at the point of the Cycle in which End fades into Beginning—the climax of the Cosmic Night is reached in the form of Absolute Rest, extending over aeons of time. Then after the aeons of Absolute Rest come the first activities of the future Cosmic Day. During the Cosmic Night, as the Aphorism states: "The LAW dwells Alone, in solitude; The Cosmos remains resolved into its condition of the Unmanifest—the Infinity of Nothingness." Then begin the first stirrings of the birth of the new Cosmic Day, which the Aphorism describes as follows: "Then comes the dawn, when The LAW superimposes the Infinity of Nothingness, and causes the Unmanifest to become Manifest; the Nothing to become Everything; Latency to become Reality; Promise to become Fulfillment." Let us consider what is meant by the words of the Aphorism.

The first step of the new activities is indicated by the words: "The Law superimposes the Infinity of Nothingness." These words, at first consideration, would seem to indicate a decided action of The LAW in the direction of "superimposing" Infinity. But such is not the Arcane Teaching. The Teachers hold that The LAW exerts no different degree or kind of power at the period of dawn, than at the period of dusk; no more at the period of high noon, than at the period of midnight. During the Cosmic Day and Cosmic Night, The LAW is unchangeable and constant in its power and influence. The difference is caused by the Cyclic Swing, or Rhythmic Movement, in the Cosmos itself, Manifest or Unmanifest. The LAW is *over and above* Rhythm or Cyclicity, or any of the Seven Laws, and is Changeless. The Cosmos, on the contrary is *under* the Seven Laws superimposed by The LAW, and is Changeable—Constantly Changing. The difference in the degree of power received from The LAW is due to the changing condition of the Cosmos, or Infinity.

In order to understand what has been said, let us imagine a mighty magnet, constant in its power, and invariable in its manifestations of magnetic force upon all within its magnetic field. Then let us imagine an Infinity of infinitesimal particles of steel-filings, separated from the magnet by a glass watch-cover. Let us suppose that owing to the operation of some unknown magnetic law, the *receptivity* of the steel particles changes in rhythmic periods, or in cyclic recurrence. In that case, it would follow that, although the power of the magnet were unchangeable and its manifestations invariable, still the action of the steel-particles would cause it to appear otherwise. For at times there would be a marked degree of power shown, and at other times a much less degree would be exhibited—but *the difference would be in the nature of the steel-particles, and not in that of the magnet.*

Or, suppose, that the Earth were to manifest varying degrees of receptivity to the Attraction of Gravitation of the Sun—then while it would seem to be a varying degree of power of the sun, the difference would really be caused by the changes in the Earth, the Sun remaining constant and invariable all the time. In these two examples, may be seen the nature of the action of The LAW upon the Cosmos, or Infinity.

Some of the occult schools who have been influenced by the Arcane Teaching, hold that The LAW is *attracted* by Infinity, or the Cosmos, just as the latter is by The LAW. In other words, they hold that there is a *mutual* attraction and effect—an action and a reaction—a reciprocal action. But this is incorrect. The LAW is *never* attracted or affected in any way by the Cosmos, or Infinity. It is Absolute and beyond mutual Relationship. Were the Cosmos and Infinity not to exist, The LAW would not vary a particle in any way whatsoever. Its Absoluteness raises it above Relations. But while this is so, the fact of the constant outpouring of the Power of The LAW causes the Cosmos to be affected by it, just as are the steel-filings by the Magnet. According to Rhythm, the degree of Power received by the Cosmos must vary—but The LAW changes not. In fact, the Seven Laws, themselves, which produce these changes in the Cosmos, are a part of the action and power of The LAW, as experienced by the Cosmos—they are superimposed by The LAW.

The Aphorism says: 'The LAW superimposes the Infinity of Nothingness." What is meant by "superimposes"? The word *"super"* means "over, or above"; and *"impose"* means "to lay or place upon." "Superimpose" means "to place upon from above," or as used in the Aphorism: "To influence from above." In other words, the Infinity of Nothingness, or Unmanifest Cosmos, owing to the influence of Rhythm and Cyclicity, begins once more to experience the active radiation of the Power of The LAW, which serves to vitalize and energize it, and thus begins the dawn of the new Cosmic Day—and the beginnings of the new Universal Life, or Cosmic Will.

In order to understand this awakening, or stirring into activity of the Cosmos, which dwells latent within the Womb of the Infinity of Nothingness, let us consider the Three Principles of the Cosmos, from which all forms, shapes, combinations and varieties of manifestation arise. These "Three Principles" are as follows: (1) The Cosmic Principle of Substance; (2) the Cosmic Principle of Motion; (3) the Cosmic Principle of Consciousness. These Three Principles are Unmanifest during the Cosmic Night, but awaken into nascency and activity with the first thrill of the dawn of the new Cosmic Day. In the end, and at the last, these Three must be considered as phases of One. But that One, in itself, is but the reflection, so to speak, of The LAW, although not by any means to be considered as being "qualities" or "phases" of The LAW. The LAW has no "qualities" or "phases"—it is over and above these things, which are but the aspects of Infinity, or the Cosmos. The Three Principles are fundamental in all manifestations of the Cosmos, from lowest to highest—from the simplest to the most complex. Wherever is found any manifestation of the Cosmos, there is and *must be* found the presence of the Three Principles in some degree of development or activity. If you prefer, you may think of the Cosmos as *consisting of* merely these Three Principles, manifest or unmanifest. These Three Principles we can never know of themselves—we know them only through and by their manifestations. Let us consider them in detail, by the light of the Arcane Teaching.

I. *The First Principle—Substance.* Substance, as the term is used in the Arcane Teaching, means the underlying "body" of things—their material quality. Everything that is manifested in the Cosmos has its "body" or material quality. Substance includes all that we may think of as Matter, in its various degrees of solidity, or lack of solidity—from the hardest steel or granite, to the most rarefied gas or vapor known to science. It includes all that science dares to think of as material body, even in the highest flights of its reason or imagination—and then all that lies beyond those conceptions. The field of substance recognized by science, as compared with the real extent of the Principle of Substance, is as no more than a hair-line drawn across a yard-stick. There are forms of matter as much more solid and dense than steel or granite, as the latter are more solid and dense than hydrogen gas. And at the other end of the scale there are forms of substance that could not be described in words, so near akin to Nothing are they. Between these two extremes there lies a bewildering number of degrees. That which science calls electricity and other subtle forms of energy, are not "energy" at all, but merely energy or motion manifesting through subtle forms of substance, which act as its body. There are forms of substance many times finer and rarer than even these. There are bodies worn by beings on higher planes which are finer and rarer than electricity. Even the ordinary Astral Bodies of beings on our own plane and stage of development, are far rarer and finer than is electricity, or the finest rays of light or magnetism. These bodies are just as real as is the piece of the hardest steel through which they may pass as easily as the X Ray passes through stone. The Universal Ether, which science assumes to be the extreme limit, and infinity, of subtle tenuity and fineness, is solid and compact when compared with many of the higher forms of substance. So much for Manifest Substance.

Unmanifest Substance is held by the Arcanes to be identical with Pure Space. In the preceding Lesson, you have seen that Pure Space is considered as Nothing. This Nothing is merely the extreme limit of the fineness or rareness of Substance. Space is not a mere idea—it is substance carried to its extreme highest limit. The Arcanes do not object to the term Abstract Substance, although they do not regard "abstract" as meaning "not." One of the old Egyptian Hierophants was once asked by the Ruler of Egypt: "What is that which would exist were there no universe; no gods; no anything?" His answer was "Space!" And this Pure Space is the Unmanifest Cosmos, in its aspect or principle of Substance.

II. *The Second Principle—Motion*. Motion, as the term is used in the Arcane Teaching, means the underlying "energy; force; or motive power" of things—their quality of action. Motion, in the Arcane Teaching is the Principle in which is gathered the cause of all that we know under the names of Energy; Force; Motive Power; Action; Activity; Attraction; Repulsion; of any and all kinds or degrees. Without Motion there could be no activities, energy or force of any kind. We are familiar with many manifestations of the Principle of Motion, such as Gravitation; Cohesion; Chemical Affinity; Electronic Attraction; Expansion; Contraction; Centrifugal and Centripetal Force; the Motive Force or Energy of Light, Heat, Electricity, Magnetism; the Energy of the Ultra-Electric Rays; etc. But these are only a very small fraction of the forms and varieties of energy and force known to the advanced students of the Arcane Teachings, not to speak of the Masters, or those on higher planes of life. There are Finer Forces not dreamt of by even the most daring scientist. Motion, like Substance, is found in each and every manifestation of the Cosmos. Wherever there is Substance there is Motion. In its highest form of manifestation Motion manifests in vibrations of such exceedingly high degree and effect that there seems to be a condition of Absolute Rest. This condition is the one existing before the first stirrings of the dawn of the new Cosmic Day. Motion is then Motionless, to all intents and purposes,—but it has not perished or been destroyed. It is Motion in Latency. There is no such thing as Absolute Rest in the *Manifest* Cosmos, but in the *Unmanifest* Cosmos there is Motion of so high a degree that it seems motionless and at rest. Thus do extremes meet, in Infinity. When the Cosmos becomes manifest, Motion decreases its rate of action or vibration, and manifestation is really a lowering in the scale of Motion; just as manifestation is a lowering in the scale of Substance. There must first be Involution before there is Evolution, of both Substance and Motion.

III. *The Third Principle—Consciousness*. Consciousness as the term is used in the Arcane Teaching, means the principle of "awareness" or "mind action" of things—their quality of mentalizing or consciousing, or becoming "aware" of other things, inner and outer. We are familiar with the form and degree of consciousness manifested in ourselves and other human beings, and we recognize different shades and degrees in this. We know a little about consciousness in the lower animals, in varying degrees. And some of us know of the degrees of consciousness in plants, in varying degrees. And, those who have studied along occult lines have become aware of the existence of mind and consciousness in so-called inanimate objects—the minerals, metals, etc., and even in the atoms—and finally in the Ether. Everything in the Manifest Cosmos has *some* degree of Consciousness. But there are many other higher and lower degrees of Consciousness, than those just mentioned. From the Unconscious-Consciousness of the Cosmic Night, when the Cosmos is conscious of Nothing, because there is but Nothing of which to be conscious; to the moment of the High Noon of the Cosmic Day, when the Cosmos is fully conscious of itself as a whole—the extreme of Cosmic Consciousness; there is a scale impossible for man to grasp by reason or imagination. There are degrees and planes of Consciousness awaiting the Advancing Ego, which transcend any possible dream or picture. The race has just begun to manifest Consciousness worthy of the name. It is just beginning to enter into the glorious possibilities of Cosmic Consciousness—it is just "beginning to begin."

And, so, when "The Law superimposes the Infinity of Nothingness," the stirrings of Manifestation are felt by the Unmanifest. The Three Principles of the Cosmos are awakened into activity—Substance, Motion, and Consciousness begin to combine and become active. There is manifested an unrest and tendency to stir into activity the latent possibilities of the Cosmos. Consciousness begins to awaken from its slumber of ages, *and strives to know itself and to realize its being.* This imparts activity to Motion, which lowers its vibrations in its effort to manifest itself. This bestirs Substance into changing degrees of being. Thus do the first indications of the Cosmic Day begin to manifest themselves. From thence onward, throughout the Cosmic Day, until its close, there is constant change of form, shape and degree of Substance; constant change in manifestation of Motion; constant change in manifestation of Consciousness.

This first stirring of Cosmic activity has been symbolized by the first stirring of the embryo within its temporary home, in which it has lain quietly since its conception. It is the first signs of the sprouting of the tiny seed of the plant. It is the peculiar, weird and mysterious light which precedes the first actual glimmer of the rising sun. Creation is beginning. The

Cosmic Will or Universal Life Principle is becoming active. The birth of the new Cosmos is approaching. The One Life is arousing itself. Infinity is preparing to become Manifest. The "o" is evolving into the ∞.

In the Manifestation of the Cosmos there is exhibited an infinitude of variety, degrees, shapes, form, and combinations of the Three Principles. It almost staggers the imagination to think of the fact that in the entire Cosmos there is never a single instance of exact duplication—*there are never two things precisely alike.* In view of this fact does it not seem folly to endeavor to make human beings adhere to a common standard—to fit into a common mould—to be cut from a common pattern?

And yet through the entire Cosmos there is ever manifest the Law of Analogy—that law which ever manifests a correspondence and agreement between all things on all planes. So true is this that if we discover certain fixed principles in one thing we may reason by analogy regarding other things, and thus discover the unknown "x" quality. "From One Know All," says the Arcane axiom. "As Above, So Below," adds the Hermetist.

And through the entire Cosmos there is ever manifest the Law of Orderly Tred. Everything proceeds according to Law and Order. There is no Chance or Disorder in the Cosmos. The Universe is governed by Law. And all things are under the Laws of the Cosmos.

And throughout the entire Cosmos is ever manifest the Law of Sequence. Events proceed in a continuous stream, ever flowing onward. No event is separate or isolated. Every event has its precedent, also its subsequent and consequent. Everything has its cause and its effect. Events compose a continuous and unbroken stream.

And throughout the entire Cosmos there is ever manifest the Law of Rhythm. Everything vibrates. Everything moves from one pole to the other—from one extreme to the opposite. Everything has its vibratory rate. Everything has its pendulum-like swing between its poles. Day is always followed by Night; Summer by Winter; Heat by Cold; Action by Reaction.

And throughout the entire Cosmos there is ever manifest the Law of Balance. There is universal equilibrium, compensation and balance. Everything has something balancing and counter-balancing it. Everything has its price. Everything has its compensation. Nature always maintains its balance. And man finds the Law of Balance always operative under the phase of the Law of Compensation. We must pay our price for everything—we cannot have our penny and our cake at the same time. We must ever pay, pay, pay. We can never get Something for Nothing.

And throughout the entire Cosmos there is ever manifest the Law of Cyclicity. Everything moves in Circles or Cycles, or Spirals. Worlds, nations, peoples, and individuals travel in cycles—the strong convert the cycles into Spirals.

And throughout the entire Cosmos there is ever manifest the Law of Opposites. Everything has its opposite pole. Everything has its other side. Everything is a paradox. Everything "is and isn't" at the same time. The Law of Polarity is one phase of this Law. In it is locked many Arcane Secrets.

LESSON V.
THE COSMIC WILL.

This is The Arcane Teaching regarding the World-Spirit; the One-Life; the Life-Principle; the Logos; the Demiurge, or that Something which men have called by still other names, but which in Truth is but the Cosmic Will from which arises all life, and action, and shape and form, and change, and appearance, and variety, and manifestation—in fact, all that we include in the term "The Cosmos." Listen to the Aphorism.

APHORISM VII. "From the bosom of the Unmanifest, arises that which men call the World-Spirit; the One-Life; the Universal Being; the Life-Principle; the Logos; the Demiurge; but which in Truth is but the Cosmic Will from which arises all life, and action, and shape and form, and change, and appearance, and variety, and manifestation. The Cosmic Will is the One which becomes Many—the Unity in which is Diversity—the First-Born from the Womb of Infinity,—the Cosmic Egg from which hatches the Universe. But this too, is under The Law."

By the term "The Cosmic Will" the Arcane Teaching designates the One Universal Living Creative Principle which has been recognized in all the great philosophies of all times and places. From the earliest dawn of philosophical thought, the great thinkers of the race have postulated the existence of a One Great Universal Living Creative Principle from which proceeded the Many. In some cases the One was held to be an Universal Being—even a Personal Being or Deity—while in others it was regarded simply as a Principle. But the underlying conception was the same—a One Living Creative Something from which the Many emerged—a Unity from which proceeded Diversity. This Universal Living Creative Principle was often confounded with The Absolute, although others held that it was subordinate. The Atlantean traditions show that those ancient people held to this fundamental idea; the Egyptians held to the existence of an Universal Life-Principle; the Chaldeans likewise; the Hindus held to the existence of the principle of Brahman, or the Universal-Life-Being, and the ancient Greek philosophers held firmly to the existence of the One Life Principle.

The Atlanteans, Chaldeans, and Egyptians held that this Universal Life Principle subdivided itself into the many forms of life and things, in obedience to an *inner law* of its being. The ancient Hindus held that the One manifested as the Many, the various schools giving different "reasons" for the manifestation as follows: one school held that Brahman manifested as the Many, in order to enjoy objective existence; another school held that *Prakriti,* the Universal Principle of Substance, was acted upon by the *Purushas,* or Soul-Principles, which it had attracted to itself, and manifestations arose by reason thereof; another school held that Brahman was merely a subordinate creative principle, which was caused to create universes by the power of Para-Brahm; another school held that all manifestation was merely an illusory dream of *Maya* (the Creative Principle), in the mind of The Supreme Being; the Buddhists held that manifestation was caused by *tanha* or "thirst," in the Universal Will-to-Live which arose from the Void of Nothingness; other schools held ideas akin to those mentioned, or variations or combinations of them.

The Greeks always held to the existence of the Universal Life Principle, calling it by various names. The very term, "The Cosmos," was used by the Stoics and others to represent the idea of the *anima mundi* or "world-soul." Heraclitus held to the "world-spirit" which he symbolized as flame. Pythagoras, in his exoteric or popular teachings taught the doctrine of the Life Principle, symbolizing it as light or flame. Other schools recognized the existence of this One Life Principle calling it "Being," a term which has persisted in modern philosophy.

By some schools, notably the Platonian, the Universal Life Principle was called "The Demiurge," the term literally meaning the "universal worker." The Demiurge was held to be an exalted and mysterious agent, by and through whom The Absolute was supposed to have created the Universe—the life of the Demiurge flowed out into manifold forms, and became the Many. This idea was adhered to by the Gnostics of the early Christian church.

The term "The Logos" was also applied by some of the schools to this Universal Life Principle. The Logos was held to be the Creative Principle of Nature, objective in the world, giving order and regularity to the universe of shapes and forms which it had manifested. This idea of The Logos was inherent in many ancient religions, and permeated even early Christianity. Ueberweg, in his History of Philosophy, says: "The Logos was a being intermediate between God and the world.... The Logos does not exist from eternity like God, and yet its genesis is not like our own and that of all other created beings; it is the first begotten son of God, and is for us, who are imperfect, a god.... Through the agency of The Logos, God created the world, and has revealed Himself to it."

In the early Christian Church there was much dispute about The Logos, but the revolution in the Church, effected by Constantine, drove it from its place of importance in the Christian theology. But, nevertheless, the idea has persisted, as witness Cudworth, the eminent English theologian and philosopher (1617-1688) who held to the existence of a "Plastic Nature," of which he claimed: "It may well be concluded that there is a Plastic Nature, under God, which, as an inferior and subordinate instrument, doth grudgingly execute that part of his providence which consists in the orderly and regular motion of matter;" Cudworth held that this idea of Plastic Nature was reasonable in view of the fact that "the slow and gradual process in the generation of things would be a vain and idle pomp, or a trifling formality, if the moving power were omnipotent; as also may be noted those errors and bungles which are committed where the matter is inept and contumacious; which argues that the moving power is not irresistible, and that Nature is not altogether incapable of being sometimes frustrated and disappointed by the indisposition of matter. An Omnipotent Moving Power, being able to dispatch its work in a moment, would always act infallibly and irresistibly, as no ineptitude and stubbornness of matter would be able to hinder such a one, or to make Him fumble or bungle in anything." The Plastic Nature of Cudworth, and his followers, was but the old Demiurge, or Logos, of the Gnostics—but another name for the Universal Living Creative Principle, subordinate to the Higher Law.

Modern philosophers and thinkers have held to this idea of the Creative Principle, regarding it rather as a Life Principle than as a Being, however. Bruno held the existence of an *anima mundi,* or world-soul-principle; others have held to the Principle of "Nature"; Schopenhauer held to the existence of an Universal Will-to-Live, which manifested its life the universe of shape and form and variety; von Hartman held that there existed an "Unconscious," or Creative Principle, similar to that of Schopenhauer's "Will"; Wundt held to the existence of an "Universal Will"; Crusius held to an Universal Dominating Will; Balzac held to a

"Universal Something, akin to Will"; Nietsche held to a "World-Will"; Maeterlinck holds to a Life Principle; Bernard Shaw postulates the existence of a Universal Creative Energy which he calls, "The Life Forces."

The Naturalistic school of philosophy postulates the existence of a composite something which it calls "Nature," which acts as the Universal Creative Energy; other thinkers speak of "Nature" in its metonymic sense, as "The agent, producer, or creator of things; the powers which carry on the processes of creation; the powers concerned to produce existing phenomena, whether in sum or in detail; the personified sum and order of cause and effect." Spencer postulates the existence of an "infinite and eternal energy, from which all things proceed, . . . which transcends our reason and even our imagination." In short, this Universal Living Creative Principle or Life-Principle, is found, under one name or another, in nearly all of the leading philosophies or schools of thought, ancient or modern. The highest reports of the human reason agree in this conception and postulate.

But the true philosophic conception must be distinguished from that of Pantheism, which at first thought seems to be the same. Pantheism claims that this Creative Principle is Deity; God; or The Absolute—that Deity and Nature are identical—that the Universe is God, and God is the Universe. Herein lies a great error, which true philosophers and true occultists vigorously oppose. The idea of an Absolute—of an Omnipotent, Omniscient (all-powerful; all-wise) Being—being compelled to work Its way up gradually, haltingly, with mistakes and stumbles, is absurd. Cudworth (quoted a moment ago) makes this point clear. And to claim that an Absolute Being is trying to "gain experience" in this way, is ridiculous. The idea that the Absolute is "trying to accomplish something" by the universal manifestation, is illogical—*for if It has not been able to reach its goal in all the past of Eternity, It can not reach it in all the future of Eternity, for the one is equal to the other.* Moreover, the Absolute must of necessity be self-sufficient, and can want nothing to perfect Itself. In short any attempt to postulate The Absolute; God; Deity or other Supreme Thing as being the struggling, striving, evolving Creative Energy, must end in failure or an illogical conclusion. It is only when it is assumed that this Creative Energy is subordinate to and ruled by an Absolute Sovereign Power, that it becomes logically thinkable. Pantheism, actual or implied, is illogical—even the idea of a Personal Deity is far more logical than is pure Pantheism. The Absolute and Nature can never be the same, try as men may to make it appear possible. Nature must always be relative, and subordinate to a superior and sovereign Power or LAW, and *the latter must be The Absolute.*

Pantheism wears many masks and disguises, and is the underlying idea of many modern systems bearing high-sounding names. Any system which is based upon the idea of an Absolute which manifests as a relative—or of a Supreme Being which manifests as Nature, and natural things, is but Pantheism, though perhaps subtly disguised. Beware of this insidious error of thought. Apply these test-questions to any system, to puncture the bubble of Pantheism, if such is contained within it: (1) *Why* does your Absolute Being depart from Its absolute nature, and become relative, manifold, and divisible? (2) *How* can The Absolute lose its absolute nature and become relative? (3) *What becomes of* the absolute nature of The Absolute, when the latter transforms Itself into the relative? (4) How can the *Unconditioned* take on conditions and limitations? (5) How can the *Immutable and Changeless* manifest change? (6) How can the Indivisible divide and separate itself into parts? And if the teaching in question postulates in Absolute *Being,* the quality of Omniscience or Absolute Wisdom, ask also this question: (7) *How can the Omniscient All-Wise Absolute Being lose Its wisdom, and display the comparative ignorance of the relative forms?*

There are but two possible logical explanations of the Absolute and Relative, as follows: (I) That the Cosmos *has no existence except in the imagination* of The Absolute Being—either as a dream, meditation, reverie, or deliberate dramatic representation, lacking all reality; or (II) that the Universal Creative Principle or Energy is *not* Absolute, but is subordinate to a Sovereign LAW. The first is the answer of certain Idealistic schools of Philosophy—the second is the answer of the Arcane Teachers of Atlantis, Chaldea, Egypt and Ancient Greece. Take your choice! But if you choose the former, then you must admit that The Absolute *deliberately and wilfully* creates the illusion *for no reason except its own pleasure* (for no real result or gain is thinkable in such case), for it is ridiculous to hold that The Absolute could be *subject to* Illusion, Ignorance, or Maya, for if such were so it would no longer be the Absolute. In either case Pantheism is "escorted to the frontier." Do not be deluded by Pantheistic subtleties, or casuistic false reasoning. Pantheism at best is but a half-truth—the other half lies in the recognition of the ABSOLUTE LAW.

The Arcane Teaching holds that the Cosmic Will—the first-born of the Womb of Infinity—the Cosmic Egg from which hatches the Universe—is in its last analysis, SPIRIT. By "Spirit" is meant "ESSENCE"—remember this definition. "Essence" is a term derived from the Latin word, *"esse,"* meaning "to be." Therefore Essence (or Spirit) means the "beingness" of Being. Spirit is the *essence of* the *Cosmos.* Spirit is that which is the first-born of the Infinity of Nothingness—the first *thing* to BE. And from Spirit all the Cosmos proceeds—and at the last the Cosmos is all Spirit. Back of Spirit there is naught by the Infinity of Nothingness. And over and above Spirit there is naught but The LAW. Spirit is Being; and Being is Spirit.

The Arcane Teaching uses the term "Cosmic Will" to indicate the creative activities of Spirit. Spirit is the essence of the Cosmic Will—the Cosmic Will is the outward activities of Spirit. But Spirit and the Cosmic Will are the same thing—in its the inner and outer aspects. By "Will" is not meant that human quality called "will"—this latter is but the mental quality *which calls forth Will.* Will is the principle of all activity—it is activity *in itself.* Life is one of the manifestations of the Cosmic Will. Will is the "lifeness" of Life. Will is the outward aspect of Spirit.

In the Cosmic Will are inherent the "Three Principles," *viz.,* Substance; Motion; and Consciousness. In the infinitude of manifestation of these Three Principles by the Cosmic Will is found the explanation of the Cosmos or Universe. In their play, and interplay, is found the secret of shape, form, variety and degrees of Substance, Motion, and Consciousness. And from these arise LIFE. Therefore, in considering the Cosmos, in its activities and manifestations, we may now forget the deeper and more subtle metaphysical and philosophical terms which we have been compelled to consider—and, instead, let us see in universal operation and manifestation, a LIVING UNIVERSE or COSMIC LIFE PRINCIPLE, ever moving, changing, flowing, evolving, proceeding, desiring, attaining, seeking, accomplishing. This is The Cosmic Will of the Arcane Teachings possessing all the attributes and qualities of the Universal Being of the Pantheists, except that of Absoluteness; for greater than the human imagination can conceive it though it be, yet it is subordinate to, and ever under, THE LAW.

In this teaching regarding the Cosmic Will, the Arcane Teaching gives us an intelligible explanation of that most perplexing idea of the One Life, or Universal Life, which has appeared in various guises and under various names in the philosophies of all times and peoples. That all Life, in the end, is One—that the individual lives are but manifestations of, and centres in, One Universal Life, has been the Truth taught by some of the greatest teachers of the race—the illumined of all ages. The majority of the schools make the fatal error of ascribing to the One Life the nature of The Absolute. The moment this is done the thinker is confronted with the paradox of the Absolute becoming Relative—a logical impossibility. The best modern thought is fast coming to an agreement with the original Arcane principle that the Universal Life is *not* Absolute—*not* Independent and Self Governed—*not* Sovereign Power—*not* God, in the highest sense of the word; but instead is Relative, Subordinate, and *under The Law*. The Arcane Teaching that the Universal Life is *not its own law,* but is under Law and governed by Laws, is the only explanation consistent with the highest report of the reason—the highest form of Logic—and the experience of science, based upon observed facts.

One of the greatest and most glaring of the fallacies of Pantheism or allied systems of thought, is that which assumes that The Absolute or Deity is "trying to" accomplish something—either in the direction of "gaining experience," or "building up" some great universe by continual progression. The idea of an Absolute, which must be Perfect, *desiring* anything other than it has is illogical. The idea of an Absolute Pantheistic Deity who must be All-Wise, trying to "gain experience" or *learn something* by playing the game of Many Parts, is childlike and ridiculous—surely an unworthy role to attribute to an Omniscient Deity. The idea of an Absolute or Omnipotent Deity "trying to," or *endeavoring to* build up universes by slow and arduous labor belongs to the category of child-thought. To think of such a Being doing "day work" is ridiculous—and then *what could He gain by it,* this Perfect and Self-Sufficient Being? And the fact remains that if all past Time has not been sufficient to accomplish perfect results, then all future Time will fail to accomplish them—for just as future Time has no ending, past Time has no beginning, *and existed forever.* And then, what did this Creative Being do in all the Eternity before Creation, if it be held that Creation had its beginning in time?

At the last analysis, the report of the illumined of the race will be found to agree with the highest report of the human reason—the report that the Universal Life can be but Relative; governed by a Sovereign Absolute Law; and subject to the Laws of Rhythm and Cyclicity—having its Ebb and Flow; its Action and Reaction; its Rise and Fall; its Days and Nights; its Periods of Creative Activity, and Creative Rest. And the Arcane Teaching squares fully with these requirements—for it is founded on Cosmic Truth.

LESSON VI.
INVOLUTION AND EVOLUTION.

In order to understand the Arcane Teaching regarding the processes whereby the Cosmic Will manifests in the universe of life and action; shape and form; change, appearance, and variety; let us seek the wisdom of the Aphorisms. Listen to the Aphorisms:

APHORISM VIII. By the Law of Analogy the Manifest Cosmos may be known. "Ex Uno disce Omnes"—From One know All. Like unto a WORLD-BRAIN" is the Cosmos. Its brain-substance is the Substance-Principle; its thought-energy is the Motion-Principle; its Mind is the Consciousness-Principle. Its will is the Cosmic Will. Its spirit is the Cosmic Spirit. Its laws are the Seven Laws. Its Sovereign is The Law.

Many philosophies have held that the universe is *mental,* in its last analysis, and that the Universal Mind is the reality behind the appearances. Others have held that the universe is merely an imagination, illusion, or dramatization, in the mind of a Supreme Being. But all of these conceptions use the terms "mind" or "mental" as something having no connection with material substance, the latter being an illusion. But the Arcane Teaching recognizes Substance as being as real and actual as Mind or Motion—the three being but aspects of the same thing—the Three Principles which are really One. And in giving to Substance and Motion equal places with Mind, the conception is seen to be rather more like a "World-Brain" than a "World-Mind," for like the brain it contains the principles of Substance, Motion and Consciousness. Thought is the product of these three—the action of Consciousness upon Substance, by means of the vibrations of Motion. As in the human brain, so in the Cosmic Brain—"as above, so below; as below, so above." From One know All. Substance and Motion are not illusions—they are co-equal with Mind, in reality and actuality. There can be no Mind without Substance and Motion; there can be no Substance without Mind and Motion; there can be no Motion without Mind and Substance. The "Three Principles" are always found together—in Everything the Three are found. There is no separateness in the Three Principles—there are, and must be, always in combination. And this combination in the Cosmos, gives us that which may be called the World-Brain.

Aphorism IX. In the World-Brain of the Cosmos arises and is manifested all natural phenomena. All natural phenomena is but the perpetual action and reaction; combination and re-combination; distribution and redistribution; of the Three Principles, in the World-Brain, by the Cosmic Will. As in the human brain material changes of form, shape, combination, character, and degree, result from mental activities—organic structural changes accompany mental states—states of consciousness are embodied in forms of material brain substance—so in the World-Brain, by the Cosmic Will, do Thoughts become Things; Desires take on Material Form; Ideas become Manifested; Mental Images become reproduced in the Material and Physical Forms, Shapes, and Appearances. Mental States precede Material Form—Mental Images precede Materialization.

In this Aphorism is contained a marvelous scientific truth, little suspected by the majority of thinkers. Every mental state produces a corresponding material change in the structure and substance of the brain—the brain-cells respond to the faintest mental state. The Arcane Teaching informs us that the Cosmos, being a great World-Brain, is governed by the same laws—"as below, so above." This being so, we may see how the Cosmos *while still being mental* may yet manifest in actual material and physical forms and phenomena, under the direction of the Mind. There is Mind back of every material and physical form and appearance. Here is the reconciliation between mentalism and materialism—idealism and naturalism. Read the above Aphorism carefully, a number of times—it contains the key of the material Cosmos, and the secret of Mentalism. Read between its lines. It informs you *why* and *how* Thoughts become Things—Mental States produce Material Forms—Mental Images cause Materialization. Here is the Key to unlock many Occult Doors. Can you use it?

Aphorism X. What men call "Matter" is but the countless centres produced by Will in the Substance Principle, through the action of the Motion Principle. What men call "Force and Energy" is but the action of the Motion-Principle upon the Substance-Principle, induced by the Will. What men call "Thought" is but the action of the Will upon the Consciousness-Principle, employing the Substance and Motion-Principles in the operation. In every action of the Cosmic Will all Three Principles are employed and involved, in varying degrees and combinations. The Will is the Motive Power behind all manifestation in the World-Brain of the Cosmos.

The above Aphorism states that which some of the more advanced of modern scientists and philosophers now hold to be a proven fact. Science and Philosophy is fast approaching a meeting point, where they will see that behind the activities and phenomena of the universe there is to be found a Cosmic Will manifesting in the multitudinous variety of shape and form; life and action. Science and the Arcane Teaching agree upon this point. As a celebrated philosopher-scientist said: "The material universe is but the outer wrapper behind which is hidden a spiritual creative activity; a striving, feeling, sensing, like that which we experience in ourselves." Conation (the voluntary power impelling to effort) is held by Wundt to be the fundamental essence of this activity. Thus Wundt postulates the existing of a Cosmic Will, similar to that of the Arcane Teaching. A recent paper by an English scientist says: "There is but one substance, and that is Spirit. Matter, so-called, is nothing but *rigid places in spirit*" Matter is now known to be but combinations of the *ions* or electrons, which are held to be little more than "centres of force" in the ether. Thought without *thinking-substance and motion* is held to be unthinkable. Likewise science now holds that there is life and mind in all material substance, from atom to protoplasm. Science like the Arcane Teachers, finds the Three Principles, Substance, Motion and Consciousness in everything. And science is beginning to see in "energy and force" the evidences of "something akin to conation." "Conation" is "the voluntary power impelling to effort; the faculty of voluntary agency," etc.; or as Mill said: "Conation, in other words, is Desire or Will." So that science is meeting the Arcane Teaching face to face, on level ground. The symbol of the "World-Brain" is sure to come into general use in the science of the future.

And now for the inevitable question—the question which punctures the philosophical and metaphysical bubble of the Pantheists: "*Why* does this Cosmic Will manifest this energy, activity, desire, longing, striving, seeking and evolution?—what is the *necessity* of it all?—what is the end sought for? As difficult as this question may be—and though it has repeatedly been styled "unanswerable"—the Arcane Teaching does not shrink from its consideration, but gives the logical and only answer, *for the answer exists*. Listen to the Aphorism!

APHORISM XI. The Cosmic Will, as the World-Brain, seeking Consciousness through its appropriate Principle, manifests the natural phenomena of the universe. From a state of Unconsciousness, through many stages of Semi-Consciousness—through many degrees of Simple Consciousness; Self-Consciousness; Super-Consciousness; and states still higher in the scale, undreamt by mortal mind, on toward the highest states of Cosmic Consciousness—Spirit conscious of Itself; the Cosmic Will proceeds. Consciousness, in all of its phases, proceeds through Change—Consciousness depends upon Constant Change. Consciousness always produces Activity, and manifests Motion. Consciousness always manifests objectively in Change and Motion in Substance—in substantial shape and form. In this, then, is to be found the explanation of the phenomena of the involution and evolution of the Cosmos, with all the incidents thereof—in this is found the answer to the Ultimate "Why."

The above is one of the most important of the Basic Aphorisms—the one which explains the "Why" of the Manifest Evolving Cosmos. The answer is understandable only through the symbol of the "World-Brain." The Cosmic Spirit or Will, awakening from its sleep of Unconsciousness, during the Cosmic Night in the Infinity of Nothingness, seeks Consciousness. Consciousness is the "livingness" of Life—therefore *the Cosmos seeks Life itself. The Cosmos manifests in order to gain Conscious Life.* Like the mortal awakening from a profound sleep, almost death-like in its intensity, the Cosmos begins its task of *regaining* Consciousness, which is the "livingness" of its Life. And as to the mortal sleeper, such Consciousness comes to it slowly.

In order to fully appreciate the meaning of the Aphorism, we must regard the nature and meaning of "Consciousness." Consciousness means "awareness," and, of course, is purely mental in principle. The Aphorism says: "Consciousness in all of its phases, proceeds from Change—Consciousness depends upon constant Change." Is this borne out by modern psychology—let us see! The best authorities in modern psychology agree to this statement. To them, Consciousness is a stream of changing mental states, with their corresponding physical changes. The text-books say: "Every act of consciousness involves a change from a past state to a present." A leading authority says: "Consciousness is in constant change";

also: "No state once gone can recur and be identical with what it was before"; also: "Consciousness does not appear to itself chopped into bits. ... It is nothing jointed; it flows. A 'river' or a 'stream' are the metaphors by which it is most naturally described. In talking of it, let us call it the stream of consciousness." Another authority says: "Consciousness results from perpetual change. It is impossible to maintain a uniform conscious state. A uniform sensation of pressure becomes quickly unnoticeable—the pressure must perpetually vary or the sensation will cease, and this is true of all conscious states whatsoever." All the best authorities agree in the above position. The Cosmic Will which is embodied in the Cosmic Substance, just as is the will of man embodied in his brain-substance, must constantly manifest changes within that substance in order that it may be Conscious. It must do this constantly and perpetually, else it becomes Unconscious. When it is remembered that states of consciousness are always accompanied by corresponding material and physical changes—that thoughts become brain-things—then we can see the explanation of the constant change in the physical world, which we call natural phenomena.

The Aphorism also says: "Consciousness always produces Activity, and manifests Motion." Modern psychology also bears out this statement. Prof. William James has brought out this point most forcibly in his works. He says, among much else on the same subject: "All Consciousness is Motor"; also: "Using sweeping terms and ignoring exceptions, we might say that *every possible feeling produces a movement,* and that the movement is a movement of the entire organism, and of each and all its parts. ... In short, a process set up in the centres reverberates everywhere, and in some way or other affects the organism throughout, making its activities either greater or less." Is it not plain that, granted the existence of the Cosmic Will in its aspect of a World-Brain, then *every state of consciousness within it must produce activity and motion* within it; and *must also manifest the corresponding physical and material changes in its substance and organic structure?* Does not this, coupled with the fact that *consciousness depends upon constant change,* give us, in the words of the Aphorism, "the explanation of the phenomena of the involution and evolution of the Cosmos, with all the incidents thereof?" Does not this explain to us the workings of the Law of Sequence?

This then is the cause behind the involution and evolution of the Cosmos as told by Modern Science. In awakening into Consciousness the

World-Brain creates centres of material shape and form within itself. Then by slow degrees more complex forms and combinations appear. Upon the created worlds appear the material appropriate for the manifestation of organic life. Then Life, as we know it, appears. Then higher forms come. Then man. Then, as on certain of the worlds, being much higher in the scale than man, appear. And then on, and on, and on, ever in an ascending scale of Life and Being; shape and form; combination and degree.

In the World-Brain, there are many planes of consciousness, just as there are in your own brain-mind. There are the instinctive planes, and those still below—the sub-conscious, and those above—and the super-conscious, and other stages of which man does not as yet dream. Just as the various braincells perform their several functions, varying in the degree of importance and function—so do the various centres in the World-Brain play theirs, in the same varying importance and degree. Each is a part of the All. And there is a relationship and interdependence between all. None is alone and separate. Separateness is an illusion. All is One. The part played by Man—by YOU—in this great Cosmic Drama, will be considered in the succeeding parts of this series of lessons. Therein will be taught the lesson of "Man, Know Thyself!"

In considering the World-Brain, do not make the mistake of the average student, in thinking merely of this speck of dust called the Earth, as being all that is included in the Cosmos. In the Cosmos are contained an infinitude of infinitudes of universes; of suns, and planets. Space itself must be exhausted before the universes are exhausted. Number itself must be exhausted, before their number is exhausted. Remember, they are the products of Infinity, and consequently *their number, degrees, and variety is infinite in extent and possibility.*

Nor, should you make the mistake of explaining of the Cosmos in the terms of Time, except as a convenience in thinking. Conceptions of finite time or space have no place in the consideration of the Cosmos—that is, the mind is unable to think of a period of time sufficiently great to cover even one phase of the Cosmic Process. The Cosmic Day is unthinkable in figures. The highest figures possible to the mind of man would not represent the year periods involved in a single second of the Cosmic Day. We are still in the Dawn of the Day, and yet that which men would call an Eternity has passed in the present Cosmic Day. Thought fails us. We are dealing in terms of Infinity. The Symbol is ∞.

In this lesson we have heard the answer to the Ultimate Question of the "Why" of the Cosmos. We have seen that that Answer is "Necessity and Law." It is the Law of the Cosmos that the Cosmic Will should *desire and will to live;* and, that in order to live, Consciousness (the "livingness of Life") is necessary; and that in order to gain consciousness, continual and constant change is *an actual necessity.* And this constant change produces the phenomena of the Manifest *Cosmos.* In a nutshell: *The Cosmos manifests in order to Live—and it Lives because Life is a Necessity of its nature under the Laws, and subordinate to The Law.* This is the Arcane Answer to the "Unanswerable Question" of the philosophers of the schools.

And in the Arcane conception of the World-Brain of the Cosmos, we have another great fundamental truth stated in simple terms, and by a familiar symbol. The human-brain has its analogy in the World-Brain. In this Arcane Teaching we may understand the principles of the embodiment of mind in matter, and the action of mind upon matter by means of energy. Compare this Teaching of the World-Brain with the teachings of science, in its phases of Inorganic Evolution, and Organic Evolution, and see how the Teaching throws light on the whole process. See how there is ever a mental action preceding the physical manifestation. Desire ever precedes function, shape and form. Mind is always embodied in substance. Substance always contains mind. The building of the crystal; the growth of the animal form from the single cell; the evolution of the chicken from the creative cell in the egg; all these are manifestations of physical action, structural change, and substance moving in response to mental inner causes. From One, know ALL. The Law of Analogy is ever manifest in the Cosmos—"As Above, so Below; as Below, so Above."

The conception of the Cosmic World-Brain also throws much light upon many phases of mental, psychic, and occult phenomena, in which the world is now taking such a decided interest. If Thoughts become Things in the Cosmic Brain, then following the Law of Analogy it is possible for Thoughts to materialize in Things on other planes of activity. The same principle is involved—the principle of mental creative activity. This is the Secret of Mentalism. This is the Key to Psychic Phenomena. This is the Explanation of Occultism. With a Cosmos, *mental in its nature,* with energy and substance; matter and motion; all receptive, responsive, and plastic and obedient to MIND—what cannot be accomplished by those who understand the Laws of Mentalism? With WILL as the great creative power in the Cosmos—what is not possible to him who understands the Art of Willing. With DESIRE as the great Creative Energy, can we not see why Desire should be harnessed, controlled, directed, guided, mastered and employed in our lives, careers and destinies?

Apply these various conceptions of the Arcane Teaching to the various philosophical and metaphysical problems which have puzzled you—and see how many tangles it straightens out; how many inharmonies it reconciles; how it brings order out of the chaos of conflicting theories, dogmas and teachings. The Arcane Teaching is a Disturber of teachings—but it is also the great Reconciler. It is the Chemical of Truth, which clears the waters of Thought.

PART III. THE LIFE OF THE EGO.

Lesson VII. The One and the Many.
Lesson VIII. Metempsychosis.
Lesson IX. Survival of the Fittest.

The Arcane Teaching

LESSON VII.
THE ONE AND THE MANY.

We now invite you to consider the important philosophical problem of The One and The Many, as explained by the Arcane Teaching. In the philosophies which hold that The One Life is the Absolute, this problem is unexplainable, for it is impossible to conceive of the Absolute, which is immutable and indivisible, changing and dividing itself into parts, or apparently doing so. With the recognition of the fact that the Cosmic One Life is not the Absolute, but is under LAW, then the difficulty vanishes. Let us listen to the Aphorism:

APHORISM XII. Know ye, that in Truth, there is but One Life and not many lives. Separateness is but relative and partial—illusory—the creative fiction of the Cosmos. Who teaches otherwise, errs. In the Cosmic Will there is the One Life in which, and by which, is manifested the Many.

In the previous lessons we have seen that the Cosmic Will is the "lifeness" of all Life, just as Consciousness is its "livingness." Back of, and under, all manifestations of Life, there is always the Cosmic Will. But the Cosmic Will precedes the particular manifestation that we call "Life," for it existed before Life appeared in the Cosmos. The great Cosmic energies and activities which manifested in world-building in all its phases, were but manifestations of the Cosmic Will bestirring itself. The fundamental activities show but little evidence of what we call Life—there seems to be but little Life in the mineral kingdom—but still the Will is seen in operation there, building up and tearing down; arranging and rearranging; combining and recombining. The attraction and repulsion of the atoms (and of the particles composing the atoms) shows us that the Will is present and in operation in these lowly manifestations. In Gravitation, we see a wonderful evidence of the operation of the Cosmic Will. In Chemical Affinity and Molecular Cohesion we have similar evidences. In all the great Natural Laws, in evidence throughout the Cosmos, we may see the operation of the Cosmic Will, always. The laws of Physics demonstrate clearly the existence of some great Conative power, animating, energizing, and manifesting in every part and particle of creation. One must indeed be a blind materialist to fail to see ever at work that "Something Within" manifesting as the "Something Without." The building up of the crystal, from liquid to regular and exact geometrical form, should be sufficient to convince anyone that there is a "Something at work" in it. Even the materialist is forced to recognize these facts—and he *does* recognize it, and calls that Something by the name of "Nature." We have no quarrel with names—if the term "Nature" suits you, use it by all means. But if you think clearly, you must recognize that your "Nature" is Conative, and acts and manifests as a Cosmic Will.

These fundamental activities and manifestations of the Cosmic Will or One Life, are akin to the activities and manifestations of our own lives. Stop to consider that your body was built up from a single cell by your Live Forces—not only your fleshy parts, but your hair, nails, teeth, and even the hardest bones which form your framework. And, likewise, the flint-like shell of the clam, oyster, and other hard-shell animals were so built up; not to speak of the harder geometrical crystal forms of the diamond and other minerals, which are but "built-up" shapes and forms. The diamond is composed of carbon, which is but a gaseous substance which becomes solid under certain conditions. The hard ivory of the elephant's tusk was built up from cells, by the Life Forces within the animal itself. So you see that Life can build up *hard substances* as well as soft ones. And the same force that builds up these hard substances, builds up the rocks and hills, and mountains, and minerals that form *the body of Nature.* Just as certain functions of the animal or human brain manifest in building up the body of the Cosmos.

The Cosmic Will from the beginning has sought to *embody* itself in objective form, in order to manifest Consciousness, which is the "livingness" of Life, as we have explained in a previous lesson. Like the Life Forces in any being, it first concerned itself in providing a *body* for itself, in order that it would have a substantial foundation for further and higher manifestation of its Life. In the Cosmos the material plane of activity is the one first operated upon. Then comes the slowing down of the vibrations of Motion, and the Principle of Substance produces the elementary particles which, combining, form matter. Then matter begins to evolve into higher forms, until at last there is produced the combination in which is possible the manifestation that we call Organic Life. From the lowly living cell-like creatures in the slimy depths of the primeval ocean-beds, arise step by step, slowly, tediously, painfully, arduously, and haltingly, but surely and steadily, form after form of higher and still higher living organisms. The modern scientific theory of Evolution—which, however, was antedated some twenty-five hundred years by the Ancient Greek Philosophers—tells us a true tale of the slow rise and development of life forms.

At last Man—a poor, weak, brutal creature with wonderful possibilities, was evolved by the One Life in its urge toward Conscious Life. And this poor creature has advanced wonderfully. And Evolution does not stop here—for Man is but an intermediate step. On other worlds in the Cosmos, there are beings as much higher than Man, as man is higher than the earthworm. Our planet is but one of millions upon millions of millions of worlds, in which Evolution is at work. We are away down low in the scale of worlds and being. There are beings as great as man's conceptions of the gods of old, dwelling on some of these planets and worlds. Some of us have dwelt on these brighter spheres, but have been sent back a grade or two in order to complete tasks left undone; or to gain experiences necessary; or because the fires of material desire had not yet died out in us, and we needed to "get enough of it" once more, in order to be free of the dross. There are planes of Life so transcendentally grand and exalted, that Man's wildest imagination cannot conceive of them. And, on the other hand, there are worlds lower in the scale so sunken in materiality and foulness, that the orthodox hell would be preferable to them. Man goes where his desires take him. He travels the road of his desires and thoughts. He makes his own route—he guides his own vessel. Man is his own Destiny.

The Many Lives are but Centres of Life in the great One Life. Separateness is but the "creative fiction" of the Cosmos—illusory and relative. All Life is but One, in its fundamental nature. The entire Cosmos is but One Life, in which we are parts or centres—in its Being we "live and move and have our being." The One Life is not far away, but is all around us, and immanent within us. While one phase of the Cosmic Paradox shows the individual to be but an infinitesimal unit in a stupendous whole, the other phase shows the individual to be identical with the Whole—connected with all by spiritual bonds and links—and sharing the infinite possibilities of the All. The life of the individual is not bounded by his personal limitations, but includes the life of the All. In this understanding and recognition there is found the reconciliation, unity and agreement between the contradictory phases of life and the universe. True spiritual advancement depends upon the increasing recognition and identification of the individual with the All.

An important point in the Arcane Teaching is that which holds that *the Cosmos is, and can be, conscious only through and by means of the various centres of consciousness within itself.* Without these centres of consciousness within itself—the consciousness of You and I and all the rest—the One Life would be unconscious. Just as the individual can be conscious only through his stream of units of consciousness, so can the One Life be conscious only through its stream of centres of consciousness. Destroy these centres of consciousness, and the Cosmos once more is resolved into its condition of Unconscious Nothingness. And, moreover, the One Life can *live* only through its centres of Life—the centres called You and I, and the rest. Will is the "lifeness" of Life—Consciousness is the "livingness" of Life—and the individual is the centre of both Will and Consciousness, and therefore of Life. As the Cosmos advances in the Cosmic Day, there is manifested a constantly increasing blending or unification of the various centres of Life—a constantly increasing identification of the individual with the All. And, thus is accomplished the approach to the Cosmic High Noon, when the One Life, *as one life and consciousness,* lives, wills and is conscious. Before that time comes, the illusion of Separateness is manifested—the "creative fiction" of the Cosmos operates in working out the approach to Cosmic Consciousness.

Thus it is seen that the Cosmos, or One Life, does not manifest as separate units of life in order to amuse itself, or to try experiments, or any of the various "explanations" hazarded by philosophy, metaphysics, or theology. It manifests through the centres, *because it must do so in order to live and be conscious.* Creation and the Universe is not a matter of whim, unreasoning desire, or arbitrary fiat of the One Life of the Cosmos. Far from that. It is the Cosmic Necessity. Just as you must *live* in order to be alive so must the Cosmos manifest Life in order to *live* and be conscious. Just as you find the imperative demand for life within yourself; so does the Cosmic Life find the imperative demand for Life within itself. The One Life is under the LAW, just as you are under the Laws. The urge of "Must" is ever impelling it forward. It is not Free—it is under the LAW and The

Laws. The LAW is ever over and above it—the Seven Laws are constantly in operation within it. The One Life is not a cruel, arbitrary master or ruler. It is your Greater Self, and subject to the same laws which govern you. *It is doing the best it can,* for itself, and therefore for you. When the individual realizes this fact—the fact that the One Life is doing the best it can; is bound by the Laws as much as is the individual; that there is no manifestation of arbitrary desire, or unreasoning whim in the Cosmic machinery; that One is All, and All is One; then there appears a *reason* and explanation for much in life which has hitherto defied explanation or reason; or theory of justice and equity. Then is there seen an explanation of that apparently arbitrary, despotic manifestation of power, which caused old Omar Khayyam to utter his rebellious protests, and cry aloud:

> "Into this Universe, and 'Why' not knowing,
> Nor 'Whence' like Water willy-nilly flowing;
> And out of it, as Wind along the Waste,
> I know not 'Whither,' willy-nilly blowing.
> "What, without asking, hither hurried 'Whence'?
> And, without asking, 'Whither' hurried hence!
> Oh, many a cup of this forbidden Wine
> Must drown the memory of that insolence!
> "A moment guessed—then back behind the Fold
> Immerst of Darkness round the Drama rolled,
> Which for the pastime of Eternity
> He doth himself contrive, enact, behold.
> "We are no other than a moving row
> Of Magic Shadow-shapes that come and go
> Round with the Sun-illumined Lantern held
> In midnight by the Master of the Show.
> "But helpless Pieces of the Game He plays
> Upon His Chequer-board of Nights and Days;
> Hither and Thither moves, and checks, and slays,
> And one by one back in the Closet lays.
> "The Ball no question makes of Ayes and Noes,
> But Here or There as strikes the Player goes;
> And He that tossed you down into the Field,
> He knows about it all—He knows—He knows."

Many daring thinkers who setting aside "the bribe of heaven and threat of hell" have dared to look Life in the face, have been overcome by a sense of impotent subjection to an arbitrary Being who, *being able to* remedy conditions, and *knowing of* the pains of mortal life in the universe, nevertheless has deliberately imposed such conditions upon living things. Such thinkers find it impossible to reconcile the claimed qualities of Love and Good in such a Being, with the manifestations of apparent injustice, inequity, pain and suffering which made pessimists of great souls like Buddha, Lao-tze, and the writer of the Koheleth or Ecclesiastes. Indeed, viewing Life from this viewpoint, one finds it hard to escape the conviction which inspired the bitter words of old Omar, when he cried:

> "What! out of senseless Nothing to provoke
> A conscious Something to resent the yoke
> Of unpermitted Pleasure, under pain
> Of everlasting Penalties, if broke!
> "What! from his helpless Creature be repaid
> Pure Gold for what he lent him dross-allay'd;
> Sue for a debt we never did contract
> And cannot answer—Oh, the sorry trade!
> "O Thou who didst with pitfall and with gin
> Beset the Road I was to wander in,
> Thou wilt not with Predestined Evil round
> Enmesh, and then impute my fall to Sin!
> "O Thou who Man of baser Earth didst make
> And ev'n with Paradise devise the Snake:
> For all the Sin wherewith the Face of Man
> Is blackened—Man's forgiveness give—and take!"

But with the dawning knowledge that the One Life, or World-Spirit, is *not* The Absolute, but is under LAW and Laws superimposed upon it, then we have a picture of an Universal Being which suffers with us and through us; rises with us and through us; strives with us and through us; attains with us and through us; rejoices with us and through us; conquers with us and through us—and whose Life is composed of our lives; whose consciousness is composed of our consciousness. Such a Being is seen to be, at the last, *one with ourselves,* instead of an outside power—and consequently, such a Being is seen to be eternally making for Good—making for *our* good, for we are one with itself. Such a Being is seen to be but the Composite Self of all the individual selves of the Cosmos—the Real Self. And in the recognition of all this, our bitterness must die away, and a great feeling of compassion, sympathy, understanding and love must be manifested by us—and felt by us. Then must come that sense of Oneness with the All which is the great reconciler—which harmonizes the Opposites, and establishes the Cosmic Balance.

This One Life is YOU—and You are it. Centres of Life, apparently separate are we now—but steadily growing toward that time, phase and state of Cosmic Consciousness, in which the All shall know itself as One—and the One know itself as All. As the Ego progresses through the stages of Spiritual Evolution, its consciousness enlarges and expands, including more and more of the Cosmos within it as the Self, until the stages of Cosmic Consciousness are reached in which the Ego finds itself blending into the Whole, and the All blending into the Self. This is what is meant by Cosmic Consciousness; Spiritual Consciousness; Transcendental Consciousness; the Higher Consciousness; the *Moksha,* of the Brahmans; the *Nirvana,* of the Buddhists; the Union with God, of the Mystics; the Divine Marriage, of the Sufis; the Brahmic Splendor, of the Oriental poets—of all those transcendental states of Consciousness, in which the Self blends into the All, in varying degrees according to the development of the soul. This is the Secret of the Mystics of all times and lands—this the Mystery of Buddha—this the Divine Bliss of the Brahmans—this the "Wine" of the Sufi symbology. Even old Omar, in his bitter complaint, was true to his Sufi instincts, and recognized the One:

> "Whose secret Presence, through Creation's veins
> Running Quicksilver-like eludes your pains;
> Taking all shapes from Mah to Mahi; and
> They change and perish all—but HE remains."

And this was the thought that inspired these striking lines from an unknown poet:

> "Thou great Eternal Infinite! Thou great Unbounded Whole!
> Thy body is the Universe! Thy spirit is its soul!

> If Thou dost fill Immensity—If Thou art All-in All—
> Then I'm in Thee, and Thou in Me, or I'm not here at all!
> How can I be outside of Thee, when Thou fill Earth and Air?
> There surely is no place for Me outside of Everywhere!
> If Thou art ALL, and Thou dost fill Immensity of Space,
> Then in Thy BEING do I dwell, or else I have no place.
> And if I have no place at all—what am I doing Here?
> Beyond the All I cannot Be—outside of Everywhere!
> Then truly in Thy SELF am I—and Thou must be in ME;
> Or else there is no All-in-All—no Me, nor Thee, to BE!"

This ONE is the great Cosmic Spirit—Cosmic Will—Life Principle—One Life of The Cosmos—in which the Arcane Teachers find the Real Self and Universal Being. This is the great Principle of Life and Being, in which "we live, and move, and have *our* being." This is the great Cosmic Life which awakens in the Dawn of the Cosmic Day, and thence proceeds gradually to evolve into the Cosmic Consciousness of High Noon; thence on to rest in the ecstatic state of transcendental Bliss, Consciousness, and Being—*sat-chit-ananda,* the Hindus call it—the Kingdom of Heaven, other mystics have called it—during the Afternoon of the Cosmic day, which state extends over countless aeons of time; thence passing into the dream-like slumber of the Twilight of the Cosmic Day; thence on toward the resolution into the state of Unconsciousness in the Infinity of Nothingness of the Cosmic Midnight; thence on to the Re-awakening at the first glimpses of the Dawn of the new Cosmic Day. As Above, so Below; as Below, so Above! From One, Know All!

Thus is the Great Cycle of the Cosmos—thus the Working of the Laws. And, ever over all dwells The LAW, unchanged, peaceful, undisturbed—ever the same—Alone—Absolute.

LESSON VIII.
METEMPSYCHOSIS.

It is not our purpose to enter into a discussion of the world-old and world-wide doctrine of Metempsychosis, Re-Birth, Reincarnation, or Re-embodiment, or by whatever other name it may be known. The modern world has awakened to a new knowledge of this ancient doctrine and truth, but in learning it is has absorbed much error with the principle of truth. We shall not attempt to *prove* the doctrine of Metempsychosis. All true occultists know that every soul which ever has experienced re-embodiment or rebirth *has an intuitional assurance of the truth of having lived before, some time, some where*—an assurance perhaps dim, but still persistent. Those who have not this inner assurance in some degree have never experienced rebirth, although they may have rebirth awaiting them after the present earth life. To those who have not this inner assurance, it is folly to attempt to *prove* Metempsychosis—at the best they will receive it merely as one of a number of idle speculations on the unknowable hereafter. To those who have the inner assurance, in some degree, no other *proof* is necessary, although explanation and teaching regarding the same is eagerly sought after. In this, and the following lesson, we shall ask you to consider the Arcane Teaching regarding the details of Metempsychosis, Reincarnation, and Re-birth. Many of the points of the Teaching may seem strange and startling to those who have studied other teachings—but careful study and comparison will show the Truth in spite of the contradictions from without. For the first point, listen to the Aphorism:

APHORISM XIII. Know ye this first Truth of Metempsychosis: The Ego is evolved from the Personal Self. Every living thing possesses a Personal Self, but even among men, many fail to reach Egohood. Egohood is earned, not bestowed as an universal natural gift. Many personalities are born, but few Egos are evolved. Personality perishes in the Astral World, after the death of the physical body—Egohood persists in Re-embodiment and Rebirth.

This startling truth, embodied in the Aphorism, is one of the fundamental principles of the Arcane Teaching. The majority of religions and philosophies have held to the idea of the universality of immortality, although there have been some notable exceptions to the rule. The Arcane Teaching however has always held that Egohood (with survival and re-birth) is conditional and exceptional. It has held that there must be earned and evolved an Ego, before that Ego may persist in Re-embodiment and Re-birth. Many of the ordinary teachings regarding Reincarnation hold that there is a continuous chain of Rebirth or Reincarnations from the lowest form of animal life (and often still lower) to that of advanced Man and beyond. This is *not* so held in the Arcane Teaching. The Arcane Teaching holds that there is Physical Evolution from the very lowest life forms to the highest (up to a certain advanced stage to be noted hereafter), but that Spiritual Evolution begins only when the Ego is evolved from the Personal Self of some creature on the plane of humanity, or some plane equal to it in other worlds. From thence on there is Spiritual Evolution, and Metempsychosis, Re-birth or Re-embodiment, which latter continues until the Ego passes through that stage and thenceforth pursues its Spiritual Evolution without the necessity of Rebirth. Most positively does the Arcane Teaching deny that YOU, the Ego, as a soul, have arisen by steps of Spiritual Evolution from the various soulstages of the animals. The Arcane Teachings also hold that the majority of human beings on earth to-day have not developed Egohood, and are therefore not likely to be reborn or re-embodied, but will, after a period of life in the Astral World, in their astral bodies, again die and fade away, being resolved into their original elements in the Cosmos.

All living things have Personality, and are able to distinguish between "Me and Not-Me"—between their personal selves and the things of the outside world. But only a portion of the human race have developed the phase called by psychologists, "Self Consciousness," or "The Sense of Individuality," in which they are able to distinguish between the "I" and the "Me." By the "Me" is meant the things of personality—the body, the mental states, the feelings, the desires, the characteristics of personality, etc. By the "I" is meant that transcendental Something in oneself which is able to stand aside and apart *and view the "Me" as from outside*—that something which enables one to feel, "I AM"—that Something which enables one to know that he is superior to the body, or the personality, and that he will always be "I AM" no matter in what part of the Cosmos he may be, or after how many aeons of time he may say it. It is most difficult to describe this phase of consciousness, but those who have it will recognize it, and those who have it not will likewise realize the lack. Some may not recognize it under the term Ego or the "I Am," but will understand when we say it is that which may be called "Soul Consciousness"—that is, a consciousness that You *are* a Soul, inhabiting a body and using a mind—a Something over and above personality and mortal life—a Something destined to live on, and on, and on—a Something which *feels and knows* that it IS. A great many people do not recognize this Something Within them, but instead *believe* that they *have* a soul, or *will have* one at least—their idea of "soul" being something that will emerge *from them* after death. The true Soul recognizes itself as being *Now*—it can say "I Am the Soul—Here and Now!" This is Egohood in its early stages.

The Cosmic Will, or One Life, begins its work of physical evolution, working from lowly forms to higher and higher, the benefits of acquired conscious experience being transmitted through the laws of Sequence or Heredity. In this way the lower animals advanced in the scale of evolution, and Man appeared. But Man was, and in many cases is now, but a higher form of the lower animals—his soul life comes later. As Man advanced in the scale, there were evolved personalities which experienced the pangs of soul-birth. They felt the struggles of the developing Something Within, and began to realize that they were individuals—the "I Am" began to manifest itself. These individuals were not always "good" people—both poles of the opposites manifested here as elsewhere—they were simply stronger and more soulful people—people who felt the Real Self within them. Thus were the Egos evolved.

When physical death overcame these individuals, after spending their allotted and usual time in the Astral World, and sinking into the astral slumber preceding the usual astral dissolution and final death, these Egos awoke to a new life in new bodies—Metempsychosis in its earlier stages. Each Ego was reborn into a new body, along the lines of its general character and desires, although it preserved but a faint memory of its past life. The Ego preserved its Character, however, although its Personality had slipped away from it. Thenceforth these Egos proceeded along the lines of Spiritual Evolution, in connection with Physical Evolution—and thereby the One Cosmic Life was enabled to evolve and progress *along two lines* of Evolution, instead of one as before—the Cosmic Will doubled its resources. In order to see the "why" and "how" of this process of re-embodiment, or re-birth, let us listen to the Aphorism:

APHORISM XIV. Know ye this second Truth of Metempsychosis: Persistence in Egohood in Rebirth or Re-embodiment, is but the Recollection or the Memory of the Cosmic Will, in the World-Brain. As the mortal brain recollects (and thus embodies) an idea, or thing—so does the World-Brain recollect (and thus embodies) the Egos. This is the Truth of Metempsychosis, and the phases of Life beyond Metempsychosis.

To those who have deemed incapable of solution the "how" of Re-embodiment, the Truth contained in the above Aphorism will come like a flash of lightning illumining the darkness of midnight. The analogy is seen at once by those familiar with the laws of the mind and the phenomena of the brain. An idea or thing, the impression of which is in the memory (occultists claim the memory to be largely astral in its nature) is recalled or recollected, and immediately passes into the field of consciousness. And to pass into the conscious field *it must be embodied* in the brain substance or cells—it must be given an appropriate body. The Cosmic Will *remembers* the Ego in the Astral World, and in the World-Brain it again embodies it in material form. We urge you to study this carefully and thoroughly, before proceeding further, in order that you may make this great Truth your own for all time. Consider this: To be remembered by the Cosmic Will in the World-Brain, is to persist in Being—*for whatever is so remembered cannot perish so long as the World-Brain persists and exists.*

And now listen to the Aphorism, telling the third truth of Metempsychosis:

APHORISM XV. Know ye this third Truth of Metempsychosis: In recognizing and knowing the "I," the individual recognizes and knows the Cosmic Will—and the Cosmic Will knows and recognizes the individual. Egohood is mutual conscious recognition—all below this phase belongs to the sub-conscious plane of the World-Brain.

In this Aphorism is contained another remarkable Truth. It informs us that the "I Am," or "I," or "Soul" recognized by the individual, even faintly, is the conscious recognition of the Cosmic Will or One Life which is our Real Self. And, likewise, such recognition is mutual, for in it also is comprised the recognition of the individual by the One Life. When we know, recognize and realize the "One" within us; then the "One" recognizes us within itself. And thenceforth it remembers us, and our Spiritual Evolution begins. As the Aphorism says: "Egohood is mutual recognition—mutual recognition between the Individual and the All." The Aphorism also informs us that below the plane of Ego, all the life activities of the World-Brain are along sub-conscious lines—below the plane of Consciousness. In other words, the Being *in whom we are,* knows and is conscious of us, only when we are conscious of Being *within us.* The recognition is mutual in consciousness. And, correspondingly, as we advance in the great scale of Consciousness, we come into a closer recognition and consciousness of the One, and the One comes into a closer recognition and consciousness of us. Finally, at the High Noon of Cosmic Consciousness, we come to know that we *are* the One—and the One comes to know that *it is us.* And toward this is the aim and goal of Spiritual Evolution.

But not all the Egos reach this stage—many fall by the wayside, or sink into the mire. We shall speak of this in the succeeding lesson, and we mention it here merely to prevent a misapprehension.

The Arcane Teaching does not hold that ReBirth is imposed arbitrarily upon the Ego, or by reason of punishment or reward for deeds "good and evil" of the physical life; but, on the contrary, that it proceeds in accordance with the operation of the Seven Laws following the general path of the Desire and Character of the Individual. In other words, the "character" of the individual, which is composed of the sum of his experience and his desires, follows the line of the general Expression of his Desires in deciding his future embodiments and life. Desire is the strong motive force of Life, as we shall explain in a future lesson, and its urge toward expression leads him into certain channels of Re-birth. An understanding of Desire and the Will enables the individual to regulate his character so that he may practically map out his future lives instead of allowing them to be determined by Blind Desire as is the case with the majority of the race.

Nor does the Arcane Teaching hold that Metempsychosis shall always continue along *unconscious* lines. The advanced soul reaches the plane of Conscious Re-birth, after a certain stage is passed—and accompanying this comes the Memory of the Past Lives, so that Life becomes continuous in consciousness and memory, after a certain stage of progress is attained. At present, the average Ego is undergoing a stage of spiritual evolution akin to the mental stage of a child of a few years of age. The child remembers but little of its past—the happenings of a few months ago are forgotten—even the affairs of yesterday seem dim to-day. But as the child advances in years it has a better and still better remembrance of the past. And, in the same way the advancing soul develops a clearer and still clearer recollection of its past lives. The dim memories, and flashes of remembrance of the past, which many of us now have, will be succeeded eventually by a full remembrance of the details of our past lives.

Moreover, the Arcane Teaching does not hold that Metempsychosis is the final stage of spiritual Evolution. On the contrary, it holds that eventually the evolving Ego will reach the stage in which Reembodiment is no longer necessary—and thenceforth the Ego will be able to actually *create* its own bodily vehicle of life from the Principle of Substance in which it is immersed.

The Arcane Teaching also hold that Re-embodiment on this one planet continues only so long as the Ego is attracted by Earth things—when it passes beyond the attractions of Earth it rises to meet the attractions of worlds higher in the plane, and so on and on. Or, likewise, it may become so gross that it may sink to a lower level of worlds beneath our own in development. Many of us now abiding on this planet, have been drawn here by reason of having fallen from the higher estate of higher worlds by reason of our material longings. This accounts for the feeling possessed by many that they are "far from home," accompanied by dim and bitter flashes of remembrance of a brighter, happier and more glorious life on some higher plane in the past. But the lesson will be heeded, and these "lost souls" who are "strangers far from home" will follow the "kindly light" which will lead them on to home once more.

The Arcane Teaching holds that the dual-nature in individuals—the "two natures struggling for supremacy"—arise from the struggle between the "I" which is the reincarnated Ego, and the "Me" which is the Personality received along the lines of heredity, ancestral race, thought, etc. The "I" is the Real Self—the "Me" is the personality which has been inherited. The "character of the individual arises from the balance struck between the two. The weak soul allows the "Me" to bear down the balance in its own direction; while the strong soul asserts the "I," and seats itself upon the throne of Individuality.

The very fact of the existence of such a struggle between the "Me" and the "I" of the individual, shows that there must be an "I" or Ego superior to and in a measure independent of the inherited and acquired "Me." And the fact that the individual experiences this dual-nature is his proof that he has attained at least some degree of Egohood, for those of the race who lack Egohood are like the lower animals and simply follow inherited and racial desire. The only "conflict" in the minds of those lacking Egohood is the conflict between opposing desires of this kind—there is no "I" to set aside desire, or to master it by Will. The strong Ego is able to master Desire by Will—able not only to desire to will, but to *will to* will. Desire and Will are the two poles of the manifestation of "Will." Desire rules the individual, unless he masters it by Will. The Ego may assert its will over the inherited desires of the "Me" or False-Self.

Personality is connected with the physical body and its psychical inheritances, and acquired tendencies. Individuality is connected with the Ego, or Real Self, which is over and above Personality, or the things of personality. Personality is bound and tied by the relative things and persons connected with one's personal present incarnation. Individuality is free from those bonds, ties, and limitations, and soars above them in its Cosmic flight. Personality says "I am John Doe, of Akron, grocer, aged 48"; or "Mary Roe, spinster, aged 45"; as the case may be. Individuality says "I am that which I Am"—above names, and forms, and personal sheaths or vehicles.

Each Ego has been embodied in numerous personalities during the Spiritual Evolution. Old Atlantis; Chaldea; Egypt; Greece; and other ancient lands have known us. Rome, Tyre, Carthage, Babylon, Troy, and other cities of the past have been ours. We have worshipped Jove; Isis; Thor; Wodin; Baal; Pan; and many other strange gods. We have learned many lessons—we have had many defeats and many victories. And we are now emerging into a *conscious* realization of what it all means. We have reached the point where we shall have "some say in the matter." We are facing the Cosmic Adventure with open eyes, and bold hearts—we are going on, and on, and on! The dawn of the Cosmic Knowing is upon us. The light is rising over the hills, bidding us awake to the tasks of the day. Let neither Time nor Space terrify us. Let nations vanish, and worlds disappear—what is that to us? The Cosmos is our Home—all parts of Space our own—all Time ours to live in and employ. All the Time there is—all the Space there is—all the Knowledge there is—is ours to have and to hold. All this is the heritage of him who can say, and feel, "I AM!"

LESSON IX.
SURVIVAL OF THE FITTEST.

Of all the various points of the Arcane Teaching, that of the law of Spiritual Survival of the Fittest is one of the most startling, when contrasted with the ordinary teachings on the subject. Many thinkers who freely admit the existence in Nature of the law of Physical Survival of the Fittest, seem to find an idea of injustice in the correlated doctrine of the Spiritual Survival of the Fittest, although the two are but correspondences on two several planes, following the Law of Analogy. When the Teaching is examined in detail, it will be seen that not only does it conform to other manifestations of Nature, but also is in strict accordance with the fullest equity and justice. Particularly is the absolute equity and justice of the law seen, when it is perceived that the failure to survive of the Personality of those lacking Egohood is not the result of arbitrary fiat or dicta, but *is the result solely of the desire and will of the entity or "personality" itself.* The entity perishes and dissolves, *not in spite of its desires and will, but because of them.*

The lowest forms of life perish almost immediately after the moment of physical death. It is true that even the very lowest creatures have an Astral Body which survives the death of the Physical Body, but as all the desires of such creatures are bound up in their physical lives they have nothing to live for after the physical body is destroyed. Such "life" persists for a very short time in its Astral covering, for Desire fading away, the Astral Body dissolves into its original elements, and the entity perishes. As the scale of Life is ascended, there is a longer survival of the Astral Body of the creature, for its desires die more slowly, being more complex and tenacious. The Astral forms of the higher animals often persist for quite a time after their physical bodies have perished, but after a time their desires burn out and the Astral form dissolves and the entity perishes. In the case of domestic animals who have become strongly attached to their human friends, and who have absorbed "something" from the latters' love for and interest in them, the Astral form often persists for years finding great pleasure in being in the proximity of the human friends, although unseen. In this case the desire for survival is strong, and almost reaches the phase of Will.

When the scale of Man was reached by Evolution, there was but little change in the manifestation of Spiritual Survival of the Fittest, for primitive Man was but a little more than an intelligent beast. When his Astral form passed out of the physical body, it was like that of the beast— it found but little pleasure or satisfaction in life apart from the physical, for its desires were altogether along physical lines. It soon found that it "had nothing to live for," and became filled with weariness, *ennui*, and dissatisfaction, and soon found comfort in the Astral sleep which precedes Astral death. After a few years, the entity perished—*because it had no desire to live without a physical body*. And, as surprising as the fact may be to many, it is true that the majority of persons to-day have advanced but comparatively little beyond the spiritual plane of the savage. Such people are so tied to physical manifestation and sensual gratification, that life outside of the physical body soon wearies them and fills them with dissatisfaction. They set into motion the "reversal of desire"—the negative pole of the "Will-to-Live," and accordingly there begins a slow process of Astral weakening and loss of vitality, which results in dissolution and the final death of the entity. A writer reports such an entity as saying (in a communication from the Astral Plane): "The disembodied learn that the Hades of immortality is the lack of physical body." Lacking desire to continue disembodied life, and *lacking the Will of Egohood* to demand Rebirth—the entity passes away gradually. Just as people in the physical body die for lack of interest, and because they have nothing left to live for—so do disembodied entities on the Astral plane likewise die because they have nothing to live for. Having failed to develop Egohood during physical, *they have nothing left to survive* after the dying away of the Body of Desire. It is true that in rare cases, extreme love for, and by, some person possessing Egohood may develop the seeds of Egohood in a disembodied entity, on the Astral Plane and cause it to seek Rebirth. And likewise some entities develop Egohood in the Astral World, through instruction from others more advanced than themselves.

There is a great difference between the Will-to-Live of the strong-willed Ego, and the Desire to live again in the same Personality which is the only desire possible to these people who have not developed Egohood or Individuality. When one realizes the "I Am," over and above Personality, then the things of Personality are left behind, and the desire and will is simply to BE. The entity in the bonds of Personality, however, simply desires *to be and remain what he was*—his Personality of "John Doe, grocer, aged 48," being his idea of his Self. This Personality having perished, such an entity cannot find anything in itself to arouse the desire or will to persist as an "I" independent of the old Personality. There is no "I" in such a person—it is all "Me," and the "Me" is the old Personality. Try to grasp this distinction, before proceeding further—it gives the key to the situation.

It must not be understood that there is no "future life" awaiting these Egoless people, after they have passed out of the physical body. On the contrary they have a more or less extended term of life on the Astral Plane, which yields them more or less satisfaction, but which must die out in time because all the old desires have been lived-out and outlived on the psychical plane (see future lessons on the Astral Plane) *and there is nothing left to live for.* Rebirth is not known to them—they cannot conceive of it for they would think that they would in that case "be some other person," and their love of their own Personality shivers and shrinks at the thought of losing their beloved "self"(?), and so they repel all idea or desires in that direction. As we have said, they are all "Me," with no "I." The "Me" always perishes, sooner or later, the "I" alone being the Real Self. Where the "I" has not been evolved or "born," it cannot exist to persist after the dissolution of the "Me," of course.

There is seen to be no injustice or inequity in this failure to grant Rebirth to these Egoless entities. It is all a matter of their own nature and desires resulting from the same. They have no "I" which desires and wills to be reborn—consequently that which *is not* cannot suffer or be injured or deprived of anything. It is like accusing one of depriving an unconceived child of life—a meaningless statement. The "Me" of the Egoless entities passes many years—often many hundred years—on the Astral Plane, and exhausts every possibility of its nature, good and bad (see future lessons on the Astral Plane). It lives out to the utmost its possibilities—and then having *out-lived* them, it has no desire for life, or reason for continued life—*there is nothing to live.* Therefore the Spiritual Survival of the Fittest is in perfect accord with exact equity and justice. Each gets that which his nature demands and desires. One cannot be robbed of that which is not his, and which he has not and never will have.

All through Nature you may see correspondences on the physical plane of the truth that "many are called, but few are chosen." Countless life-forms are created, but few survive. The fish lays millions of eggs, but only a few fish reach maturity. Countless seeds are cast forth by the plant, but only one or two take root. This is a law of Nature, and in its operation the inequity is only apparent. The Law of Balance is preserved. One cannot be robbed of what he has not. If one has not desires, he cannot be hurt by not having the result of desires. Place the savage in a palace, and he dies broken-hearted—restore him to his jungle and he is happy. Place the hungry wild-beast in a cage and feed him well, and you break his heart. Each craves his own. There is Compensation and Balance manifested on all planes of life.

And now for a consideration of those who have attained Egohood. Is their Destiny and Progress assured? you ask. Not at all! They have simply begun to climb the ladder of Spiritual Evolution. They will mount as far as their desire and will—not a step further. They may tire of the climbing and begin a retreat. The law of Spiritual Survival of the Fittest has many phases; many planes; many stages—it is operative from first to last during the life of the Ego.

Let us suppose the case of an Ego which has not as yet reached the plane of *conscious* Rebirth. The Ego dwells for many years on the Astral Plane (see future lessons) and lives out its personal desires, and profits by its experience in so doing, for the "I" is there to learn and remember—for it has the faculty of Egohood, that of "standing aside and looking on at one's self." Gradually the personal desires and ideas are outlived, and the essence of the experience is retained by the Ego, the latter then feeling a sense of "age" and a need for rest. This is followed by the Astral Sleep, which sooner or later comes to all entities on the Astral Plane, but from which the Egoless fail to emerge, and from which they are resolved into Nothingness. But the Ego, having an "I" above Personality, *has something to survive,* and accordingly it is drawn into the channels of Rebirth, according to the currents of attraction, and again finds a physical body, this time suited as nearly as possible to the requirements of its "character." Then begins its new life on the physical, which may be long or short. Sometimes the new body is not found fully adapted to the growing requirements of the Ego—sometimes sickness or accidents cut short the new life—and sometimes the needed experience is gained quickly—and the Ego again passes to the Astral Plane, there to enjoy a period of rest and spiritual growth and assimilation, which will be manifested in a new birth later on.

But if the new life persists beyond childhood, the Ego must progress in order to attain further stages of Spiritual Evolution. If it simply lives its old life over again, without reaching forward to greater attainment and knowledge, then it is dangerously near falling into the attraction of the "descending path" which will take it down the ladder, step by step; life after life; and which, unless the Ego learns the lesson and again steps forward, will eventually cause it to lose its Egohood and become Egoless, which means eventually dissolution. But these downward steps are not in the nature of *punishment*—they are simply stages of the law of Sequence or Cause and Effect, proceeding along the lines of Desire and Will. These descending Egos follow their desires, just as much as do the ascending ones. It is *not* Reward or Punishment, in either case—it is simply Cause and Effect, and the Path of Desire. Desire is the great motive force. There are cases known of Egos descending the scale to such an extent, drawn by their material, physical and animal desires, that they have even descended to the scale of animals and eventually perished as entities, unless rescued by the love and affection of human friends who aroused in them the last flickering spark of Spirit, and thus set them again upon the upward path. These cases, however, are very rare.

It must not be supposed, however, that all persisting Egos are "good." On the contrary, there are many persisting Egos who are giants of "evil," possessed of the sense of the "I," but filled with personal desires of material aggrandizement and selfish attainment which makes them stand out above the crowd. But such, sooner or later, are taught their lesson and either change their natures or else sink to annihilation, for all real progress must lead toward the life of the One, not in the direction of selfish personal attainment and Separateness. The error of Separateness is often brought to the minds and understanding of these Egos, by their desires finally leading them to a place where they are actually *separated* from their kind, and thus they experience that hunger for human companionship, sympathy and love which results in a change in their entire nature. One has but to look at the inner lives of some of the selfish "great men" of our own and past ages, in order to see examples of this stage of experience.

And, so the evolving Ego rises in the scale—if he be Fit—and reaches higher and higher planes of life. He passes on to other worlds and universes, when he is fitted for them. He may fall back, again and again, but there is always a chance for him to regain his lost steps. Many in this Earth-world of ours have fallen back from higher planes, and suffer soul-hunger for their lost states—these will regain their lost estates, if they will but look upward and onward and live the Life. There are glories ahead of the persistent Egos which cannot be described in human words. We do not become "God" as the Pantheists hold—*but we become as gods.* There are infinite possibilities ahead for us—there is no limit to our greatness and attainment, if we are true to the Inner Light and our Real Self. Finally we reach the stages of the highest Cosmic Consciousness, in which the Cosmic Will experiences the consciousness of Itself as Itself—then do we know that We are It, and It is Us. The Cosmos becomes conscious only through the consciousness of its Centres of Consciousness—and we are those Centres. This is what Spiritual Evolution means—this is what it is for. This is why the law of the Spiritual Survival of the Fittest is operative—the Cosmos is endeavoring to develop itself to its utmost degree and stage of Consciousness. Just as do we endeavor to retain in our consciousness our best and highest thoughts, ideas, and knowledge, so does the Cosmos endeavor to remember and preserve its noblest, highest, and fullest creations. The Success of the Cosmos depends upon this—its Progress is dependent upon it—its Conscious Life renders it necessary. This is the End, Aim, and Goal of the Cosmic Evolution. And it is a worthy end and reason for all that is. The more that one enters into the spirit of the understanding of the Universal Life, the more does he identify himself with that One Life, and the dimmer and smaller does mere Personality seem. And in the end, he finds himself willing and desirous of living his life, in, through and by that One Life of the Real Self—the Cosmic Self—the "I" of the ALL.

To those who think sadly of the personalities which disappear during the course of Spiritual Evolution, we would say that careful thought will show that even *they have lost nothing.* Not only is their dissolution caused by their own desires and lack of will; but moreover, nothing is really lost. Personality is nothing but the "creative fiction" at the best—all that was *real* in those entities who dropped by the wayside is *preserved.* The One Life is all that was real in them—and that One Life persisted and survived. It was but a changing of form in the One Life. *It was not the destruction of a real thing.* It was but the discarding of a poorly fitting suit of clothes, worn by the One Life and Real Self. No one is injured—nothing is lost. The All remains the All. Personality is but the mask worn by the One. The One discards its mask, but remains Itself. Justice and Equity are not violated even in the faintest degree. The Wise see this and smile—the Unwise see it not and weep. The reflection of the sun in the falling raindrop disappears when the drop falls into the stream—but the stream remains, and the Sun still shines and is reflected in its running waters. All that Is, remains—though the shapes, and forms, and illusory appearances vanish.

The wise and thoughtful of all ages, and races, have recognized the Illusion of Personality and Separateness. Men have endeavored to escape it in many ways. The Buddhists and the German Pessimists have deemed Personal Life evil, and have devised plans to escape from the same. The Buddhists would escape by beating a Retreat and endeavoring to escape Rebirth by attaining Nothingness or *Para-Nirvana*—a Return to the Nothingness from which all came. The German Pessimists advocate a killing out of the Will-to-Live—a Cosmic suicide, so to speak. But the Arcane Teachers scorn the Retreat—they bid their students to look ahead—they sound the bugle call of "Forward—Advance—Charge!" They press forward to the Cosmic Adventure. They urge all to go on, and on, and on—until the mists of Personality disappear before the sun of the One, and the individuals find themselves at One with the All. Surely this is a more glorious way to reach the goal! It is true that in the end, the One falls again into the Sleep of Nothingness, only to reawaken after the aeons have passed—but what of that? Is it not better to advance, than to Retreat? Is it not better to be Brave than a Coward? Not to speak of the infinite glories ahead of the advancing soul, is it not "worth while" to attain Conscious Oneship with the All, rather than to deliberately choose the path of Retreat into Unconsciousness?

But to him who falls by the wayside—as well as to him who persists and survives—there is meted out an equitable reward. There is "no bribe of heaven or threat of hell" to those who Know. It is all Cause and Effect—each gets that for which he pays—each pays his price. And, finally to all comes that Peace which passeth all Understanding. There are no Lost Souls. There are None outside of the All. There is no Outside. All are included Within the One. Yea, even the last, least, and most unworthy. For there is but One!

PART IV. MOTIVITY.

Lesson X. Dominant Desire.
Lesson XI. Fate or Freedom?
Lesson XII. Sovereign Will.

LESSON X.
FATE AND DESTINY.

From the earliest days of philosophical reasoning, metaphysical speculation, and theological dogmatism, the great questions regarding Fate or Freedom have formed an important feature of controversy. In many forms, and in manifold guises, has this great question presented itself for consideration by the human mind. Backward and forward has this tennis-ball of thought been tossed, victory being claimed by all parties engaging in the game of discussion. Early philosophy was concerned with the question of Fate and Destiny vs. Freedom, and able thinkers arrayed themselves on the respective sides of the question. Metaphysics joined in the controversy with subtle and hair-splitting definitions, theories, explanations, and conceptions. Theology took an active interest in the fray, its particular tennis-ball being called Predestination, Foreordination, or Predetermination. Modern Science has now entered the field and her advanced thinkers insist upon the truth of the principle of Determination (but not pre-Determination) by Natural Laws, which applies to all branches of science, and is seen in operation in all the fields of universal activity, physical and psychical.

The Arcane Teaching holds as Truth the idea that every thing and all things—every event and all events—are governed by Law. That every thing and every event is under Law, Order, and Sequence. That there is no such thing as Chance. That every event is a link in the Cosmic Sequence of events. That every thing is a part of, and not apart from, the Whole Thing. That every event is a part of, and not apart from, the Whole Event. That nothing "happens" without precedent causal events proceeding regularly and in logical sequence. That there are no "accidents," or events outside of the regular order. Hearing these statements, the student will feel impelled to ask the inevitable question: "Is this Reign of Law, Order, and Sequence, but another name for the old fetish of Fate, Destiny, or Predestination? Are we then ruled by arbitrary Fate—governed by the decree of Destiny? Are all events Preordained, Predetermined, and Predestined?" And this question must be met—and shall be met—not ignored and evaded as is customary in so many of the teachings, philosophies, and theologies. Let us consider the matter in the light of the Arcane Teachings. Listen to the Aphorism:

APHORISM XVI. Know ye, that Fate is but the distorted image of Law, Order, and Sequence, The wise know that Fate, if existent, would be an exception to Law—a twin-error to Chance. Law there is; Order there is; Sequence there is—but Fate there is not. Fate, Destiny, and Predestination would imply the existence of Decree and Foreknowledge in the Cosmic Mind. There is no such Decree; no such Foreknowledge. When the Cosmic Mind "knows" a thing or event, it knows according to Law, and the knowing and the manifestation are simultaneous. Fate, Destiny, and Predestination, are but names for half-truths—imperfect visions of Law, Order, and Sequence.

Although to the average mind there appears to be but slight connection between the idea of Fate or Destiny and that of the foreknowledge and decree of Deity, still the former ideas have had their birth in the latter. Back of the fundamental conception of Fate or Destiny one always finds the shadowy form of some Supernatural Being who *decrees* the Fate or Destiny. In the old mythologies the gods decreed the fate and destinies of mortals, and all cosmic happenings, the details and working out of the plan being left in the hands of minor supernatural beings, such as the Parcae, Fates, or Destinies, who were goddesses believed to preside over the birth, life, and fortunes of men. In the Grecian and Roman mythologies these Fates were three in number, *Clotho* who held the spindle, *Lachesis* who drew out the thread of men's destiny, and *Atropos* who cut it off. The Supernatural Being, or beings, always promulgated the decree of Fate or Destiny. *Fate was never a matter of natural law and order, but always the working out of an arbitrary decree, or divine fiat.* This idea is seen to be correct by reference to the definitions of the terms as given by the best authorities. Consider the following definitions:

Destiny: "The power which presides over the lot or fortune of men; the fate, lot, doom, or fortune appointed, allotted, or predetermined for each person or thing; the ultimate fate of a person; etc."

Fate: "The decree of God by which the course of events is fixed; a fixed destiny depending upon a superior cause, and uncontrollable by man; appointed lot; doom; inevitable destiny; etc."

Fatalism: "The doctrine that all things are ordered for men by the arbitrary decrees of God.... It is carried out to its most pitilessly logical extreme among the Mohammedans, where everything that can happen is 'kismet', or Fate.... in theology it has given birth to theories of Predestination." (By some writers the term is used also as synonymous with "Determinism," which is the scientific doctrine of causation, continuity, etc, *from natural causes.* This usage of the term is misleading, and is historically incorrect.)

Predestination: "The act of appointing beforehand by irreversible decree or unchangeable purpose; the act of foreordaining, decreeing, beforehand, or predetermining events; the purpose of God from eternity respecting all events;" as, "God's infallible providence and predestination" (Joyce); and, "If God presees events, he must have predetermined them" (Hale); also, as "By the decree of God for the manifestation of his glory, some men and angels are *predestined* unto everlasting life, and others *foreordained* to everlasting death. These angels and men are *predestinated* and *foreordained.*" (Westminster Confession of Faith.)

So, it may be seen, that the decree of a Supernatural Being is always back of, under, and in, all true conceptions of Fate, Destiny, Predestination, etc. These ideas cannot be divorced—they stand and fall together.

One of the main points of difference between the opposing conceptions of Law, Order, and Sequence, and of Fate, Destiny and Predestination, is seen to be in the assumption and denial of the Divine foreknowledge, and decree. Fatalism holds that some Supernatural Being has foreknowledge, and exercises arbitrary decrees determining all events, including the fate or destiny of mankind, as a race and individually. The theory of Law, Order and Sequence, on the contrary discards the idea of foreknowledge, and denies the arbitrary decree and foredetermination. Instead, it holds that the Cosmic Activities, and the incidental events, proceed regularly, orderly, and in sequence, from and by reason of the operation of Natural Laws. The Arcane Teachings hold that these Natural Laws are superimposed by, and are reflections of, The Absolute LAW—the Efficient Reason of the Cosmos. The modern scientific schools of Determinism agree with the Arcane Teaching so far as the idea of determination by Natural Laws is concerned, but differ from it by holding that The LAW is but a name which may be applied to the sum total of Natural Laws.

Another great point of difference between Fatalism and the Arcane Teaching is, that Fatalism insists upon *arbitrary happenings and events,* unrelated to, and in spite of, natural law and order. Fatalism denies that preceding events have any relation to the "fated happening," and holds that the latter would have happened *in spite of any precedent event.* In short, Fatalism makes the "fated happening a thing standing apart from the Chain of Sequence—something resulting from arbitrary and independent decree. Thus, Fatalism holds that one's death, for instance, is "fated" (decreed) to happen in a certain way, at a certain time, and at a certain place, irrespective of the Law and Order of the Cosmos. Fatalism carried to an extreme shows the fallacy of the idea, as for instance the Mohammedan who refuses to allow his wound to be treated for the reason that if he is fated to die of the wound he *will* die, and if fated to live then he will recover without treatment. Or, the fanatics who refuse to run from a wild beast, on the same grounds. Or those who refuse to rescue a drowning man, lest they interfere with Fate.

The following quotation from the article on Fatalism, contained in the New International Encyclopaedia, will show the distinctive points between the teachings of Fatalism and those of the scientific school of Determinism, which latter agrees in many important essentials with the Arcane Teaching. The writer of the article says, in part: Fatalism is "the doctrine that the course of events is so determined that what an individual wills can have no great effect on that course. Fatalism must be carefully distinguished from Determinism, as the confusion of these two conceptions has been responsible for much of the popular prejudice existing against Determinism. Fatalism, as has been said, denies that Will has efficacy in shaping events. Determinism maintains that this causally efficient will is itself to be casually accounted for; this is entirely different from the fatalistic assertion that Will counts for nothing. In fact Determinism and Fatalism are fundamentally antagonistic. *Determinism asserts that events are determined by some of the events that immediately precede them; that if the latter were different the former would be different.* Fatalism *denies* that immediately preceding events have anything to do with the origination of events immediately following: *It asserts that the latter would occur even if the former were changed.* . . . To say that one's death is fixed by Fate is to deny that it takes place by natural law. Or, more accurately, it is to say that however much one varies the cause, one cannot vary the effect. . . . The fatalist's position is that the *end* is predetermined, but not the *means;* the determinist's position is that the events now occurring lead by causality to other events, which are thus fixed because their causes are actually existent. Or, to put it still another way, for the fatalist what actually determines the event is not another event immediately preceding, but *some mysterious decree issued by some mysterious agent ages before the event.* This enables us to see that Fatalism gives no scope to the will. But Determinism, which merely asserts that every event has its determining conditions in its immediate antecedents, includes among the antecedents the human Will. . . . Thus Determinism is consistent with a belief in the efficiency of Will, and Fatalism is not."

In short, Determination holds that events are *Determined*—Fatalism holds that they are *Predetermined.* The one recognizes Natural Laws as the determining power—the other holds that Supernatural Decree predetermines and foreordains.

Predestination is Fatalism carried to its logical conclusion; Predestination holds that God appoints and determines beforehand by irreversible decree or unchangeable purpose—arbitrarily and irrevocably predetermines—the events of the universe, first and last, great and small, in general and in detail. Not only the universe as it is at present, but as it must have been forever through all eternity, and as it will be forever through all eternity. If the Divine Fiat has so gone forth, then everything is predetermined, and the Eternal Universe is but an automaton registering the Divine Decree, down to the minutest detail. In this case, everything, indeed, is caused by "the Will of God."

Theologians endeavor to escape from the above conclusion by a flow of words—like the cuttle-fish they darken the waters of thought by the flow of dark, unintelligible words, and thus make their logical escape. But a plain consideration of the facts of the proposition, laying aside theological subtleties—a consideration in the light of Common Sense—shows us that admitting a Personal Deity, possessing All-Wisdom and All-Power, then Predestination must be a logical result. Let us examine the statement.

If Deity be All-Wise, (Omniscient), then he must *know* all things, absolutely, truly, infallibly—*all things,* past, present, and future. He must know the subsequent results of all actions—the subsequent effects of all causes, the operation of all laws. He would not be able to make mistakes of judgment, or errors of foresight. There could be no necessity for any changing of his mind, if his wisdom is absolute. He must possess perfect and infallible Foresight, Foreknowledge, and Prescience, which means: "The quality of having knowledge of, or foresight into, events before they take place." And if he so *knows* what will take place, and his knowledge be *true, perfect and infallible* (and it must be so to be *absolute)* then these foreseen, and foreknown, events *must* take place and occur. As Hale well says: "If God presees events, he must have predetermined them." If this be not so, then the absolute qualities attributed to Deity are false and non-existent, or the terms are meaningless.

Moreover, if the All-Wise *knows* what will happen (and this he must know if he be All-Wise) then even his All-Power cannot change the things that he *knows to a certainty.* Some theologians, wishing to escape from this dilemma, have held that his All-Power may overcome his All-Knowing, and thus take away his infallible Foresight, Foreknowledge, and Prescience—but this is childish, for Absolute Knowledge could not be destroyed, impaired, inhibited, or changed. Deity must be held to be either absolute or not absolute. If he *is* absolute, the above facts must be assumed to be correct—if he *is not,* then we must go behind and beyond him for the *true* Absolute.

Moreover, if such a Deity exists, he must have *made* the laws of the universe, for there could have been nothing else to have made them, and if they existed without his making, then such a Deity would not be absolute. If he made them, then he must have set them in motion, and kept them in motion ever since. And, if so, then he must be held responsible for all that happens, or can possibly happen, under them—they are his own creation, and he is their Cause, and the Cause of all that proceeds from them. Moreover his All-Knowing must have made him *fully aware of* all the possibilities and certain effects of the operation of these laws. There is no escape from this conclusion.

No wonder that old Omar raised his voice in indignant protest against this conception when accompanied by the "bribe of heaven and threat of hell" as a reward or punishment for doing that which must be inevitable because it has been predestined by Deity. The conception of a Personal Deity, or Personal Supreme Being, absolute in nature, who created the universe and its laws, must carry with it as a logical accompaniment the conceptions of Foresight, Foreknowledge, and Predestination—which are but newer names for the old fetish of Fate and Destiny. In this is found the paradox of theology, from which it can never escape, and which it has never been able to reconcile.

But the Arcane Teaching does not hold to Decree and Foreknowledge, either in a Personal Deity or in the Cosmic Mind. Its Aphorism denies the "existence of Decree and Foreknowledge in the Cosmic Mind." It says that "When the Cosmic Mind 'knows' a thing or event, it knows according to Law, and the knowing and the manifestation are simultaneous." For when the Cosmic Brain "thinks" or "knows" a thing or event—then the "thought" *becomes* a thing or event, and is actually manifested. The Cosmic Mind knows only what is existent, for what it knows is manifested because of the knowing. And what it knows, it knows because of the manifestation. In the Cosmic Mind, knowing and manifestation are identical—simultaneous—one. The Cosmos is the only BEING that exists and can know the Cosmic Activities. Other than itself there is naught but The LAW, which is above Being, and above Knowing, and above Action, as we know those terms. Any attempt to attribute to The Absolute the qualities, attributes, and properties of Man, inevitably results in postulating a Personal Deity, whose All-Knowledge is the Predestination of the Universe—whose will, decree, and fiat, is Fate. And in that case upon that Deity must be placed the responsibility *for everything that happens* in the universe. In that event, then indeed we may say with the poet:

"His the credit; His the blame; His the glory; His the shame."

In the place of Fatalism, Destiny, and Predestination, the Arcane Teaching offers the Orderly Trend under Cosmic Laws inherent within the Cosmos, proceeding as Law, Order and Sequence. Not the result of arbitrary fiat or decree, but the result of natural laws proceeding in regular order, as the Cosmos evolves toward Cosmic Consciousness and All Knowledge. When the Cosmos is resolved into Infinite Nothingness, then we find naught existent but The LAW. And The LAW is the only thing left upon which to fix the Final Blame—if blame there be. Fix it so, if you will. If it belong to The LAW—give to It Its own. But The LAW is no Person—no Being—It is ABSOLUTE LAW—constant, unchanging, invariable, eternal. In LAW we find the only refuge in our highest flights of thought, reason, or imagination. It is not a Law Giver—it is LAW in Itself.

The Arcane Teaching

LESSON XI
LAW, ORDER, AND SEQUENCE.

We live in a Cosmos governed by Laws existent by reason of the very being of the Cosmos and the existence of The LAW. There is no blind Chance, nor Arbitrary Decree in the Cosmos. There is no place or room for these for Law fills the whole field of Cosmic Activity. There is no Disorder, or Inharmony. Everything is in Balance. Chaos does not exist. From The LAW proceeds the Seven Cosmic Laws, which in turn are subdivided into seven; and these into seven; and so on, the septenary division and subdivision extending into the Infinitesimal. But in large and in small—and both are alike—there is ever Law and Order, Continuity and Sequence, Manifesting and in full operation.

And, over all is The LAW of Laws—Absolute—Alone!

As the mists of the morning disappear before the rays of the rising sun, so will the superstitions, fables, and dogmas be dissipated by the knowledge of universal natural law and order. In a universe governed by eternal laws and Cosmic order there is no place for the Fates; the Destinies; the Arbitrary Decrees; of the fables, folk-lore and legends, even though they be covered by the robes of philosophy or theology. Before the light of Reason, these things must melt away, when the Truth is seen, the half-truths disappear. Fate, Predestination, and dance—Threefold Error—flee before the conception of Law and Order in the Cosmos. Listen to the Aphorism:

APHORISM XVII. Know ye that, under The LAW, the Cosmos is governed by Law. Each and every thing, and all things, proceed in Orderly Trend. In the Cosmos there is no Chance; no Disorder; no Inharmony. The Three Principles: Substance, Motion, and Consciousness—are equally under law. Those who teach otherwise, err.

This statement agrees with the report of the reason of the most advanced minds of the race, past and present. Every intelligent conception of the Cosmos must of necessity include the conception of Law. Without this inherent indwelling Law, the Cosmos could not exist—the Cosmos would be Chaos. The very origin of the term "Cosmos" shows the underlying thought in the minds of the ancient Greek philosophers who first used it. The word itself is derived from the archaic Greek word *komeo*, "to take care of," and the early Greek philosophers used it first in the sense of "order," and later in the broader sense of "the world or universe, from its perfect order and arrangement, as opposed to Chaos." Its use as "the World-Soul" came later, and included the earlier conceptions. Its antithesis the word "Chaos"—has two meanings, viz.: (1) "A yawning empty space"; and (2) "Confusion; or, a mass of matter in confusion without order or laws; a confused mixed, mass, without order or regularity." In both of these usages, Chaos is absolutely opposite in meaning to Cosmos. When we postulate a Cosmos without Law and Order, we are simply applying the term to what is really Chaos—either a Nothing, or else an Orderless Universe. Order always implies the existence of Law—the two are inseparable. There can be no such thing as an universe half Cosmos and half Chaos. Order and Chaos are antithetical. Law and Chance are antithetical. One annuls the other—they cannot exist at the same time. The three Primary Axioms of Logic show us this fact. Let us consider them for a moment:

I. *The Axiom of Identity:* "The same quality or thing is always the same quality or thing, no matter how different the conditions in which it occurs."

II. *The Axiom of Contradiction:* "No thing can at the same time and place both be and not be."

III. *The Axiom of Excluded Middle:* "Everything must either be or not be; there is no other alternative or middle course."

These are established axioms of Logic. A leading authority, Prof. Jevons, says of them: "Students are seldom able to see at first their full meaning and importance. All arguments may be explained when these self-evident laws are granted; and it is not too much to say that the whole of Logic will be plain to those who will constantly use these laws as the key."

Therefore we must either hold that the Cosmos is under Law and Order, or else that it is not. And if it is not, then Chance or Arbitrary Decree rule the universe—and the Cosmos is but Chaos. There is no alternative—there can be no half-and-half about the matter. Which is it? We need scarcely to assure the student that the highest modern scientific thought agrees perfectly with the teachings of the ancient occultists, to the effect that the

Cosmos is governed by Law in every detail, and as a whole; and that there is universal order, balance, and harmony manifested through it. Not only is this so, but the ordinary human mind is able to discover the existence of Law in the universe, in its every phase of manifestation. The rising of the sun; the flow of the tides; the law of gravitation; the mechanical laws; and Natural Law in all of its phases; show the existence of Law in the Cosmos. Science shows us that the entire universe is held together by the operation of Law—that if the tiniest atom were released from the operation of Law, the entire universe would be resolved into Chaos, so interdependent are its parts, and so incompatible with Universal Law would be the slightest exception thereto. The Laws of the Universe can never be "broken"—if we come in contact with them and refuse to govern ourselves accordingly, we suffer—but the Law remains intact. We do not "break" the Law of Gravitation when we step over a precipice—we only prove its existence. If we could "break" the tiniest Law of the Cosmos, the Cosmos would be Chaos.

And these Cosmic Laws are not the result of the arbitrary fiat or *dictum* of some Being. They are inherent in the very nature of the Cosmos. There never has been a moment in the existence of the Cosmos in which twice two did not make four; never a moment in which a straight line was not the shortest distance between two given points; never a moment in which the laws of mathematics, geometry, and logic were not as true as they are today. Cosmic Laws were not *made*—they are inherent in the Cosmos, and inseparable from it. These Cosmic Laws arise from the *reflected power* of The LAW itself—they are superimposed upon the Cosmos in the very nature of the Cosmos.

The Aphorism continues: "Each and every thing, and all things, proceed in Orderly Trend." This is a statement of the Law of Orderly Trend, one of the Seven Cosmic Laws. "Orderly" means: "In order; arranged or disposed in order; observant of order or method; not disorderly; keeping order; well regulated; free from disorder or confusion; characterized by good order; according to established order or method; according to due order or method; duly; regularly; etc." "Trend" is a word derived from an old root meaning "a circle; a ring; round; etc." and its present accepted meaning is: "to move around or about; to extend or lie in a particular direction; to run; to stretch; inclination in a particular direction" or strictly: "to proceed in a particular direction." Its use in the Arcane Teaching implies a "proceeding or moving forward," and also (in the esoteric sense) cyclic progression. Thus the Cosmos is held to "trend" in an "orderly, regular, established" manner, according to Cosmic Laws, and under The LAW. Evolution is a manifestation of Orderly Trend and Sequence.

The Aphorism continues: "In the Cosmos there is no Chance; no Disorder; no Inharmony." We have seen that where Law and Order govern and rule there can be no Disorder nor Inharmony. Harmony and Balance maintain where Law and Order govern and control. We wish to add a few words regarding the subject of Chance, owing to the popular misconception of the nature and meaning of this much used word. "Chance" is generally held to be: "an accident; something happening without a cause; a supposed agent or mode of activity other than a force, law, or purpose." The word was derived from the Latin word *cadentia*, meaning "the falling of the dice." An "accident" is "something that happens suddenly or unexpectedly," but the word is generally used in the sense of "something happening without due cause, and out of the established order." The strict meaning of "Chance" is "without cause," and it is generally so used. But with the advancing knowledge of the universal prevalence of causality, Chance in the original sense of the term is no longer regarded as existent, possible, or reasonable. The word is now employed in the scientific sense of: "The unknown, or unforeseen cause or causes of an event." As Benley says: "Chance is but a mere name, and really nothing in itself; a conception of our minds, and only a compendious way of speaking, whereby we would express, that such effects as are commonly attributed to chance, were verily produced by their true and proper causes." The highest modern philosophical thought agrees with the Arcane Teaching that: "In the Cosmos there is no Chance." Where Law and Order reign, *there can be no Chance;* no "accidents" no "happenings," in the sense of "without cause." Even the cast of the dice is now seen to be as much the result of Law and Order and Sequence as is the motion of the sun, planets and tides. Casualty has been superseded by Causality in philosophical thought.

Aphorism XVIII. Know ye that each and every event, and all events, proceed in Orderly and Logical Sequence. There is always a Something Before and a Something After, which men mistakenly call Cause and Effect, but which, in truth, are but relative stages of the Cosmic Sequence.

Aphorism XVIII informs us regarding the Law of Sequence, another one of Seven Cosmic Laws. It informs us that "each and every event, and all events proceed in orderly and logical sequence." This Aphorism declares the principle of what modern philosophical thought has called the Law of Continuity, by which is meant that universal principle or law, by virtue of which there is ever maintained a relationship of precedent and subsequent—cause and effect—between all events; the idea being diametrically opposed to that which holds that events are independent and not related to other events. In the Aphorism the word "orderly" is used in the sense defined a little further back. The word "logical" is used in its general sense of "agreeing with the natural reason"; and therefore, is employed in the Aphorism, in the sense of "in a manner which accepted by the human reason as natural, orderly, according to law, and reasonable—and which therefore might be reasonably expected were the preceding events known." The word "Sequence" is used in the sense of: "A succession, or following after, in orderly arrangement and uniformity; a series of things following in a certain order of succession." The word itself springs from the Latin word, *sequens,* meaning "to follow," and the idea of *following in regular order or procession* constitutes the essential meaning of the term.

The Law of Sequence causes all things to proceed in a *continuous stream or procession of events.* "Continuous" means "unbroken; uninterrupted; connected; with no intervening space." An "Event" is a "happening; something that occurs; the consequent or result of any action." Therefore the Law of Sequence causes all happenings, occurrences, or events to flow, proceed, and evolve from previous events, happenings or occurrences; and likewise to result in subsequent events, happenings or occurrences, which flow, proceed, and evolve from them. There is always a "something before" and a "something after" every event, happening, or occurrence. Every event has *reasons,* and is in itself one of the *reasons* for that which must follow after. Just as no link in a continuous chain can escape having a preceding and succeeding link, so no event can fail to have precedent and subsequent events connected with and related to it. No event can be *isolated* from the Cosmic Chain of Sequence, or the Cosmic Stream of Events. No event, and no thing, can *stand alone* in the Cosmos. Every thing and every event is interdependent, from the very nature of the Cosmos itself. Thus we see that there can be no such thing as "Chance" or "accidents" in the Cosmos. Nothing ever "merely happens," in the usual sense of the phrase. Everything, every event, every happening, has its preceding causes, and from it will emerge the succeeding effects—all being links in the continuous chain of Sequence.

We recognize these things, dimly, in everyday life, and call them the workings of Cause and Effect. But the Aphorism makes a distinction here and informs us that that which men mistakenly call Cause and Effect, "in truth, are but relative stages of the Cosmic Sequence. Let us proceed to a consideration of this truth.

The statement of this Aphorism apparently conflicts with the accepted philosophical and scientific conception of the Law of Causation, but the difference is largely a matter of expression, and the Arcane Teaching is in full harmony with the advanced conceptions of Causation, as interpreted by the highest authorities. The Law of Causation, as advanced by modern scientific thought, may be stated generally as the conception that every thing is an effect of precedent Causes and, at the same time, the Cause of the effects which arise from it—thus each thing is a link in an endless chain of Cause and Effect. Another way of stating this conception is that every event in time, or thing in space, has Causes; and at the same time is the Cause of succeeding effects in the shape of events in time, or things in space. This conception of the Beginningless and Endless Chain of Cause and Effect is seen to be very similar to the Chain of Sequence of the Arcane Teaching. *But here is the difference.* The Arcane Teaching *does not* hold that the Chain of Sequence is Beginningless and Endless. On the contrary, it holds that the Cosmos emerged from the Infinity of Nothingness at the Dawn of the Cosmic Day—therefore, this particular Cosmos had an actual beginning in time; and likewise, it will have an ending in time, when it again is resolved into the Infinity of Nothingness. The LAW is held to be the only Eternal, using the term in its absolute sense.

The Cosmic Activities proceed according to Law, Order and Sequence. What you are today—what happens this moment—is the logical result of all *that has gone before* in the Chain of Sequence. What *is,* is not because of Chance—but in accordance with Law, Order and Sequence. What will be tomorrow—a year hence—a million years hence—will be the logical result of all the things and events that are manifesting this moment. There is no break in the Chain. Everything, and every event, proceeds from what has gone before. And from every thing, and every event, develop the seeds of future events and things. Every thing, and every event, is a blossom—and contains within itself the seeds of future blossoms. Every event is but a stage in the Whole Event of the Cosmos. Every thing is but a part of the Whole Thing of the Cosmos. The Cosmos is the Whole Thing, striving, moving, thinking, and doing, in myriads of forms and shapes and manifestations—acting in the countless series of events which together constitute the Whole Event.

At any particular moment in the Cosmic Day—at this very moment that you read these lines—certain things are at certain places, under certain conditions, acting in a certain manner—certain events are occurring under certain conditions. All this is the result of Cosmic Causes operating since the first glimmer of the Cosmic Dawn. And, likewise, at any imagined moment of the future—a year hence—a century hence—a million years hence—at any given moment there will be certain things in certain places, under certain conditions, acting in a certain manner—certain events will be occurring under certain conditions. And this too will be the result of the Cosmic Causes, operating from the beginning—operating and in existence in some stage of Sequence, today—this moment. All that *is* proceeds from all that has gone before. And from all that *is* will flow, proceed and evolve all that shall be even unto the very ending.

And these things and events are "certain," not because of Fate, Destiny or Arbitrary Decree, but because of the operation of fixed and certain natural laws, constant, invariable and immutable. There is no Fate, no Chance, no Accidents. Cause produces Effect. Everything has its precedent, and will have its subsequent. The seeds of the future exist in the present. The seeds of the present existed in the past. No thing or event is arbitrary, separate, disconnected, independent. We are all parts of a Cosmic Whole, taking part in one Cosmic Event. Can you imagine a single thing or event without precedent causes? Can you imagine a Cosmic Law being broken? The parts are conditioned by the Whole. This is not Fate, but Law, Order, and Sequence.

The Arcane Teaching

LESSON XII.
DOMINANT DESIRE; SOVEREIGN WILL.

Aphorism XVII informs us that "The Three Principles—Substance, Motion and Consciousness—are equally under Law." The leading scientific minds of the day hold that the Reign of Law is operative not only over matter and motion, but also over mind. There are but few psychologists who hold otherwise, although a few are reluctant to admit that the operations of human volition are caused, and such therefore hold on to the old dogma of "causelessness" although candidly admitting that the only other alternative is the theory of Chance. This reluctance may be explained by the influence of the old theology which held that the admission of cause in volition would annul the doctrine of "free will" (in the sense of free *choice),* and would destroy man's moral responsibility. The theologians, however, do not accept the alternative of Chance, but murmur something about "special provisions of Providence," without explaining what they mean by this. But all denials of the operation of universal law on the mental plane are in direct defiance of the modern scientific knowledge of the laws of psychology, and the common experience of the race which informs us that people act and choose because of *motives and reasons.* And all human education is based upon this understanding and principle.

The trouble with the theologians is that they confuse Law, Order, and Sequence, with the old fetish of Fate, Destiny, and Predestination. They recognize the logical absurdity of holding one morally responsible for doing what for all eternity it has been predestined, predetermined, or fated one should do. When Determination is divorced from Predetermination, a new light is seen. Notwithstanding the theological reluctance, its advocates nevertheless *act* as if psychological laws were true, in advocating the "training" of the mind, and in offering the "motives" of rewards and punishments for actions. If the volition is free, how could these "motives" influence or affect it. All education and training of the mind implies the existence of mental laws of choice and action. The "Law of Association" is but the Law of Sequence. Without Law in the mental realm, there is but the alternative of Chance—theology to the contrary, notwithstanding.

APHORISM XIX. Man on the personal plane always acts and chooses strictly in accordance with the nature of his personal character. His personal character is determined by the nature of his psychical organism resulting from heredity, environment, and experience, and consists of a collection of mental states the motive principle in which is Desire (including Fear, which is but a form of Desire). The personal man, like the lower forms of life, always acts and chooses, according to the sum or average of his desires and fears, the strongest motives always dominating and determining the choice and action.

Each man has a personal character—just as each actor in a play assumes a "character." Each character, as the Aphorism states, is "a collection of mental states." These mental states are manifest as traits, tendencies, temperament, nature, disposition, personality—what we know as "the nature of the person," in fact. Different persons are attracted by different things, in different degrees, and respond in different ways and in different degrees. No two persons are exactly alike. Each person has his own nature, disposition and character. The dictionaries say that Character is: "The personal qualities or attributes of a person." Each character has its personal collection of feelings, desires, wants, inclinations, likes and dislikes, habits of thought, capacity for thought, degree and character of will, etc. Each has its sub-conscious collection of stored up impressions, memories, inherited traits, etc., as well as its conscious mental faculties—in fact, nine-tenths of the mental activities arise from this subconscious region. Each character has its collection of seed-thoughts which constitute its share of the race experience—the experiences of its ancestors. And each has its store of impressions and experiences which have modified it accordingly. The result of heredity, environment and experience creates a personality and character according to which one acts and chooses. This character, at any particular moment, is just what a man *is* at that particular moment. And as he *is,* so will he act and choose. He always acts and chooses *by reason of* what he *is*. On the personal plane, he cannot act differently. And what he *is*—his character at the moment—always has as its motive power the sum or average of his desires and fears.

This is the point at which we must consider the objections of the "free will" theologians who will not admit that man acts and chooses according to the sum and average of his desires and fears. These people put forward the three leading "proofs" that man does not so act and choose. Let us consider them, briefly, in detail. They are as follows:

I. *That one may refuse to act on a desire or fear, however strong. He may oppose his will to the desire or fear and defeat its power.* This statement is unquestionably true, but the explanation is that in so *willing* not to act upon the desire, he is really acting upon other and *stronger* desires or fears which urge him *not to do* the thing in question. Each desire is a motive—and the strongest motive dominates and decides. Before he may will *not to act,* he must first desire or "want to" refrain from the act, or else fear to act. In short he must *want not to* more than he *wants to.* Instead of disproving the action of Desire, it affords a very good proof. He chooses to do that which he "wants to" most strongly.

II. *That one may choose to act upon a higher desire rather than upon a lower one—to act from a higher motive than from a lower one.* This also is unquestionably true—but what is the "higher desire" and the "higher motive" but *another form of Desire.* If the "higher" is stronger, it conquers—if the "lower" is stronger, *it* conquers. Whichever is felt by the man to be the *most desirable* according to his reason, experience and feelings is the strongest motive. Sometimes the scales are very evenly balanced, and it requires but a mental speck of dust to tip it one way or the other. But this does not disprove the rule—it only emphasizes it.

III. *That one has the evidence of his consciousness that he is free to act as he pleases—or to choose between two or more different courses of action. One feels most strongly that he has the freedom of choice and action.* This is the "proof" considered unanswerable by the theologians. It is undoubtedly true, so far as it goes, but a moment's consideration will show one that it adds but another proof to the truth of the power of Desire, and the Law of Cause and Effect. Waiving entirely the obvious rejoinder that the feeling or consciousness of freedom has no causal relation to the act, we see that the man merely feels and is conscious of the fact that *he may act and choose as he pleases.* Certainly he may, no one disputes that—*but why does he "please"?* Why does he *want to* do one thing in preference to another? And *why* does he finally *choose* to do one thing instead of the other? Is it merely Chance? Is there no *reason* or cause? Is it not true that he finds it *more desirable,* or *more satisfactory,* to do the one thing? Does he not weigh the motives, reasons, feelings, and desires, by the light of his own reason, experience, nature and character, and then decide in favor of the most desirable course? His *will* is free, of course—but his desires, feelings, "please to," and "choose to" depend upon elements of his character—and the strongest motive, conscious or subconscious, wins the day. Between two things or objects, one chooses that which appeals to him as the "most desirable"—that which he "wants" most, or fears least.

Many will object that if this be true, it is unjust to punish one for doing what he must do according to his character. This objection arises from the old conception of Fate and Predestination, which held that a man *must* do a certain thing, *in spite of all that might tend to prevent.* This of course would make all "punishment" a rank injustice, and an absurd proceeding. But the doctrine of Cause and Effect does not so hold. On the contrary it holds that one's character may be, and is, changed, modified and altered by the restraints placed upon certain actions. These afford new motives for action or non-action. The theory of *human* Law, at least, is not that one shall be "punished" for wrongdoing *in the spirit of wrath or vengeance,* but that the "punishment" shall act as a deterrent, warning, and *restraining motive* to prevent the recurrence of the act on the part of the criminal, and to prevent others from making the same mistake. It is society's method of protecting itself—not a system of revenge. The very fact that the penalties of the law serve to deter some from wrongdoing is but a proof that the strongest motive dominates. The birch prevents the schoolboy from misbehaving, though he so desires very much. He fears to incur punishment, more than he desires to misbehave. We may *blame* people for acting wrongly, because we regret that their characters were not better developed, or that their judgment was not more perfect. We often make the mistake of blaming *effects,* instead of *causes.* Would it be just to "blame" or "punish" if our acts resulted from Chance?

In the same way, remorse and regret mean that we realize that what we did or chose was not wise or desirable, as seen in the light of subsequent events—we regret that the higher, nobler, or wiser motives were not dominant; or feel sorrow at the results of our actions. These latter feelings are often cited by those who deny Cause and Effect on the mental plane. But what, indeed, would be the reason for regret and remorse if our actions had been decided by Chance instead of by causes? If we remove Causes, we are in the hands of Chance—would that be a desirable exchange? If we deny Law, we must attribute all actions to Chance!

Summing up the fact of Dominant Desire, it may be said that people act in accordance with *the line of the Greatest Satisfaction*. This Greatest Satisfaction depends entirely upon the nature of the person—his character—which is regulated by his tendencies, disposition, inherited qualities, results of his experience, environment, education, training, history, etc., all of which, of course, have other causes behind them. Whatever gives to the person the Greatest Satisfaction evident at the moment of action or choice, that will he do or choose. This is the rule—test it most rigidly by applying it to your own acts and decisions, and those of others. But in so testing, do not overlook the effect of Habit as crystallized Desire; nor the effect of Fear as negative Desire. When two desires are otherwise equal, the one most habitual will win the day. The element of Fear, or Aversion, is but a Desire "not to," or "to avoid, or get away from." Compulsion by others may result in action through Fear. And one often refrains from manifesting a desire *because he fears to* "*pay the price.*"

Did you ever make a choice, or perform an act which gave you the *Least* Satisfaction, or which you knew to be the *most undesirable* under all the circumstances of the case? If you did so—*WHY did you do it?* If you yield to the suggestions, desires, reason or will of another person, against your own inclination and judgment—what is this but the "line of the least resistance," which gave you the least trouble or dissatisfaction at the moment, and in which the negative Desire of Fear had its effect? In the case of hypnotic influence, or the domination of one's will by another by any means, the rule is not broken, for the stronger person's will influences and arouses the Desire of the weaker person. Even in this case, desire or fear is the motive of action or choice.

In considering this subject, remember that the Aphorism says "the sum and average of his desires—the strongest motives always dominating and deciding the choice and action." We often are forced to "strike an average" between our conflicting desires. And then again, wisdom, experience and intelligence enable us to discriminate between the *desirability* of objects and acts, and thus play an important part in the choice. And imagination gives us a wider range of choice, by presenting a greater number of objects before us for choice. But wisdom, experience, intelligence and imagination result from Causes.

A Dominant Desire always has for its motive the attainment of something which will bring the Greatest Satisfaction, immediate or remote, or the prevention of something which will bring dissatisfaction, immediate or remote—either to the person himself, or to others in whom he is interested. Aversion, fear, or the tendency away from persons or things, are merely the negative phases of Desire, and come under the same rule. The "most desirable" thing, according to the judgment of the moment, is always chosen—the "most undesirable" thing of the moment is always avoided. Sometimes this necessitates "striking an average." So in the end we do that which we *"like to"*—we do what we *"want to"* do most. The "want to" and "like to" arise from Cause, and are under the Law of Sequence—links in the Cosmic Chain of Eventuality.

And so, the nature of one's character determines his acts. This explains many actions in a strange way. For instance, one man is kind because it gives his nature the greatest satisfaction; just as another gains the greatest satisfaction by being otherwise. One finds satisfaction in doing his "duty"; while another finds satisfaction in escaping it. One finds satisfaction in virtue; another in vice. One finds it in selfishness; another in doing for and giving to others. One finds more satisfaction in giving his life for his country; another finds it in running away and hiding. One finds the greatest satisfaction in giving; another, in getting. One finds the greatest satisfaction in being moral; another in the reverse. One takes the greatest pleasure in being a good citizen; another finds his satisfaction in the opposite. Each acts according to his nature and character—just as a cat and dog acts according to its nature. But man can change his nature, *if he so desires*. And he often so desires, while the lower animal does not—that is the main point of difference.

We have laid much stress upon this subject of Dominant Desire, because we wish to awaken you to a realization, perhaps for the first time, of what an important part Desire plays in the choice and actions of the man on the personal plane of life—how much in thrall to it is the race. When one realizes his bonds, he is in a position to work to rid himself of them. It is only when the slave realizes that he *is a* slave, that thoughts of freedom come to him. There is a plane above that of Personality—a plane in which Positive Will takes the place of Desire. Sovereign Will is above Dominant Desire. Listen to the Aphorism:

APHORISM: XX. When man attains Individuality—Egohood—he enters upon the plane of Will, and rises above the plane of Desire. Desire and Will are the opposite poles of the same Principle—the Centre of Balance being Reason. On the plane of Will, though one still remains under Law, yet he may learn to use Law instead of remaining passive to it. He may learn to oppose law to laws. He may learn to create Desire by Will, as well as to restrain and master Desire by Will. Furthermore—and this the greatest of all—he may learn to WILL to Will. He may learn to complete the Circle of Will. He may learn the Secret of the Excluded Middle. When this last Secret is learned, man is well on the road to Mastery.

By rising to the plane of Will, over and above the plane of Desire, we rise above the lower laws, and acknowledge supremacy only to the higher laws. We may then oppose Law to laws, and counteract and use them. Desire and Will are but the opposing poles of the same principle—Reason being the Centre of Balance, as the Aphorism states. The majority of the race remain centred in the negative pole, few reach the centre—and still fewer learn the secret of swinging the centre over to the positive side. He on the negative plane can do no more than to Desire to Will. He of the positive plane may learn to WILL to Will He who has learned the secret may transmute his desires, and transform his inclinations, tendencies, and tastes. Such a one is the Master of Desire, instead of its slave. The art of WILLING to Will is one of the great feats of occultism—one of the great attainments of the Arcane Teachings. In it lies also the secret of Will Power in its outward manifestations, for he who can change, and *create* desires in himself, can produce similar results in the desire-mind of others. In attaining the plane of Positive Will, one enters into the field of all Occult Power and Attainment—the rest is all a matter of progress, practice, exercise and mastery. When one grasps the Secret of Will, he has laid hands upon the Sword of Power.

Running back from cause to prior cause, and to still more remote precedent causes of his desires, the Individual finds himself at last confronting the Cosmic Will. Retracing his path back to the present, he finds himself confronting his Personal Will, which is moved by Desire. In other words, he finds a Chain of Desire extending from the Cosmic Will to the Personal Will—a chain of countless links, but having a beginning in Will, and an ending in Will—an Endless Chain, because it is a Circle. Thereupon he learns the first lessons of the Arcane Secret of the Excluded Middle, and thenceforth strives to realize *the union of the two ends of Will.* From the realization of this Union arises the Individual Will—the Positive Will of the Ego. In this process the law of Cause and Effect is not violated, but WILL is made the Cause of Will—the Cause and Effect merge. When this is attained—then does Man indeed become the Master!

PART V. THE ASTRAL PLANE.

Lesson XIII. Lower Astral Planes.

Lesson XIV. Astral "Black Keys".

Lesson XV. Higher Astral Planes.

The Arcane Teaching

LESSON XIII
LOWER ASTRAL PLANES.

There are three great planes of manifestation in the Cosmos—the Material Plane; the Astral Plane; and the Spiritual Plane. There is much confusion in the use of the term "plane" in the occult writings, for it is employed in various ways, from necessity and in the absence of other words with which to express the unfamiliar facts of the case. For instance, many occultists very properly speak of "the physical plane; the mental plane; and the spiritual plane, of Thought," meaning respectively thereby: (1) the plane of thought connected with the sensations of the body, the physical desires, etc.; (2) the plane of intellect, reason, etc.; and finally, (3) the plane of the higher mental activities and manifestations, familiarly known as the Spiritual Plane of Thought. The beginner in the study of occultism is apt to confuse the above usage of the term with that employed in speaking or writing of the Three Great Planes of the Cosmos, the Material Plane; the Astral Plane; and the Spiritual Plane; the second of which, the Astral Plane, will form the subject of consideration in the present lesson, and the two immediately following it in sequence.

The word "plane" has been appropriated by occult writers, from necessity, and given a meaning apparently at variance with the accepted usages. In ordinary language a "plane" is a "perfectly level, flat, and smooth surface." In geometry and astronomy it is sometimes used in an abstract or ideal sense, to indicate "an ideal surface supposed to cut or pass through a solid body or in various directions; as the *plane* of an ecliptic, the *plane* of a planet's orbit, etc." It is also used in a figurative sense, implying "a level, or field" as "on the plane of reason; on the plane of common sense, etc." Generally speaking, its figurative use implies a layer, strata, or *level*, and it is used in occult phraseology in the figurative sense of a level, or strata of Cosmic activity or manifestation.

But the student is cautioned against confusing the term "plane" with any conception of "place." A plane is not a place. A particular place may include several planes, and sub-planes; for the planes interpenetrate each other. A plane has no dimensions in space, and rather more resembles *a state or condition*. It cannot be measured in the three dimensions, and yet it is capable of measurement by degrees in the Scale of Vibrations. These states or degrees of vibration interpenetrate each other, without interference, in which peculiarity they have correspondences or analogies in physical phenomena. For instance, a dozen or more currents of electricity may pass along the same wire, at the same time without interfering with each other, and may then register each on its special instrument, providing that the rate of tension or vibration be different in each case. Or, again, light vibrations, heat vibrations, vibrations of electricity and magnetism of several degrees, vibrations of the X-Rays, sound vibrations, etc., may manifest and remain present in the space of a room, at the same time.

The various planes of manifestation blend into each other, and each of the three planes has seven sub-planes, which in turn are sub-divided into seven minor planes, and so on, until seven times seven acts of sub-division have been made.

On the Physical Plane of the Cosmos occurs the various manifestations of the physical world—the world of matter and energy. It is the plane best known to us, for all of our physical activities are performed on some of its sub-planes. On these planes there are manifestations of matter of degrees unrecognized by the senses of man, as well as the familiar forms and degrees. Likewise there are forces and energies of which man of to-day is totally ignorant, with the exception of a few advanced souls who have risen above the ordinary race limitations. It is not our purpose to enter into a consideration of the Physical Plane in this lesson. Neither is it our purpose to enter into a consideration of the Spiritual Plane, the conception of which is beyond the comprehension of the ordinary human, and which the words of the ordinary plane of life would be utterly inadequate to express. Our subject for consideration here is simply the second plane of the Cosmos—the Astral Plane.

The term "astral" (from the Greek word meaning "a star") is of ancient usage in the occult teachings. Astral "regions" and Astral "beings," were held to be places and beings of a more ethereal and finer order and degree than our material world and beings—so far as the bodies of the latter were concerned, at least. In the Astral regions the disembodied entities and the supernatural beings were held to abide. The term was often used loosely and in a manner tending to confuse the student. In fact, even to-day the term is used with various shades of meanings, by the different schools of occultism, and confusion results by reason thereof. Some schools use the term "Astral Plane" to designate only the *lower* sub-planes of the Astral, using other terms to designate the *higher* planes, which latter they often confuse with those of the Spiritual Plane. Others include the entire series of above-the-Material planes, lower and higher Astral and Spiritual alike, under the general term of Astral Plane. The Arcane Teaching follows the most approved ancient usage, and applies the term "Astral Plane" to the intermediate plane of the Cosmos—the plane lying between the Material and the Spiritual—including, however, the higher as well as the lower Astral sub-planes. Such has always been the custom of the Arcane Teachers, and it is, moreover, in accordance with the most ancient and authoritative practice.

There are many sub-planes on the Astral Plane, many of which bear close analogies to corresponding planes known to us on the Material Plane. There are also sub-planes containing life activities, which are different from the more familiar ones, and which bear the same relationship to the latter *that the black keys on the piano-board bear to the white keys.* On these "black-key" sub-planes dwell entities strange to human sight and thought, but which, nevertheless, form a part of the universal manifestation of life. These entities are non-human—never were human, and never will be human. Their evolution has been, and will continue, along totally different lines. Occultists group these entities under the general term of "elementaries," or "elementals," although their degrees and characteristics vary greatly, one from another. We shall consider these entities in the following lesson.

Beginning our consideration of the Astral Plane, we must not fail to take notice of one of the subplanes nearest the material—the sub-plane in which the Thought Currents operate, and also in which the Astral Bodies of the embodied, and the Auric Colors are visible. On this sub-plane the phenomena of Mentalism manifest. This sub-plane is the one nearest to the ordinary Material Plane, and is often penetrated, unwittingly, by persons whose psychic faculties have become sharpened and who have developed the qualities of Clairvoyance, Astral Sensing, etc.

It is scarcely necessary to explain in detail the facts relating to the Astral Body of human beings, for the student is supposed to have had some preliminary acquaintance with the general subject of occultism. We shall merely note the general facts in passing. The Astral Body of the person is the finer body, or inner envelope, of the entity or soul. This Astral Body has long been known in the traditions of the race, and has been called by various names, such as "the ethereal body"; the "fluidic body"; the "double"; the "wraith"; the "doppelganger," etc. It is composed of Astral substance, which is much finer than the matter with which we are familiar. It bears the same relation to ordinary matter that steam does to ice. The Astral Body leaves the material covering, or ordinary body of the person, at the death of the latter. It also often wanders far from the physical body when the latter is sleeping. Under certain conditions it may leave the physical body during waking hours, and project itself to distant points in space. The familiar "apparitions of the living" are instances of this travel in the Astral, and the phenomena of Clairvoyance is largely due to this form of Astral manifestation. The Astral Body is invisible to the ordinary physical senses, although those possessing Clairvoyant power, or well developed Astral Senses may see it plainly. It may also lower its vibrations and "materialize," as above noted, at which times it becomes visible as a shadowy form apparent to the ordinary physical senses. During the life of the physical body, however, the Astral Body is always connected with the latter by a thin, slender filament, which if broken results in the death of the physical body. Contrary to the ordinary teaching, the Astral Body is composed of seven "sheaths" or "layers" of substance, the grosser of which disintegrate or "sloughs off" when the entity rises to higher Astral sub-planes, and which must be again "materialized" when it revisits the lower planes.

The Aura and Auric Colors of the Astral Body are in the nature of emanations or radiations from the Astral Body, which are manifested in some degree by every person, and which recent scientific investigation has proven conclusively, by means of photographs, etc. The Physical Body, even, has its aura of vitality vibrations, or "Vril," which flow freely from it, particularly when the vitality of the person is strong. This "Vril" is the "human magnetism" of the magnetic healers, and others, and which serves to arouse strength and vigor to those to whom it is applied. The Astral aura, on the contrary, is rather an emanation of the mental states, feelings and emotions of the person's mind. It is egg-shaped, and extends on all sides of the person to a distance of about three feet. It manifests various colors, particularly around the head, the colors corresponding to the character of the mental states being manifested, or those habitual to the person. For instance: Red indicates the animal passions, lust, anger, etc. Blue represents religious emotion, etc.—light blue denoting what is generally called "spirituality," but which in reality is but an ethereal, refined form of religious feeling. Spirituality is more a matter of knowledge and life development, rather than feeling or emotion. Green denotes jealousy, and, in one of its shades, that which is generally called "tact," "agreeableness," "diplomacy," or in its lower forms, "deceit." Gray denotes selfishness. Yellow, intellectuality in its various degrees and forms. Black is the astral color of hate, malice and vengeful emotion. Persons in whom the faculty of Astral Sensing is well developed may see these auric colors plainly, and are thereby informed as to the mental characteristics of the person under observation.

On this lower sub-plane of the Astral are also manifested the thought waves, thought currents, thought-forms, etc., which are manifested in the phenomena of Mentalism. Thoughts and mental states manifest in objective form. The person manifesting active thought or feeling, emanates waves and currents of thought-force which spread around him in constantly widening circles in every direction. In this way great thought-clouds are formed which hover over and around places to which they are attracted. Thought-clouds of the same general character have a tendency to coalesce and mingle and blend with each other, and to move toward persons, places and localities in which similar thoughts or feelings are being manifested. The Law of Attraction operates in this direction of drawing thought influences toward those who are manifesting similar thought vibrations. Cities, towns and smaller places—even places of business, office-buildings, houses, and rooms have their own particular thought atmosphere, which may be felt by those sensitive to such influences, and *seen* by those possessing the faculty of Astral Sensing.

Akin to these thought-clouds are what are known as thought-forms, which are thought-clouds of great density and power of cohesion, which are also charged with the strong Will or ardent Desire of the persons emanating them—and which are often practically *vitalised* by the "Vril," or vitality of the person, which has been infused into them. Such thought-forms often exert nearly as great a psychic power over those with whom they come in contact as would the sender himself, in person. They are akin to the desire-elementals mentioned in the following lesson.

These thought-clouds and thought-forms abide on the lower sub-planes of the Astral until they finally disintegrate. They tend to coalesce and gather around places in which the vibrations are harmonious to their own. Some places have their mental atmospheres of vice, others of greed, others of industry, others of the reverse. In short thought atmospheres exist everywhere on this lower Astral sub-plane, just as does the material atmosphere exist everywhere on the material plane. One is just as real as is the other. They have all the correspondences which one might expect. Those who are able to travel in the Astral Body find this thought atmospheric phenomena a source of never failing interest, although at times one is glad to will himself away from some of the scenes, so gross and base are the emotions and feelings manifesting in the dark, heavy suffocating clouds of thought force—so horrible some of the thought-forms. But even these may be driven away by an exercise of the Will, and thought-vibrations of a contrary nature tend to repel them and scatter them away from one's vicinity.

On a sub-plane of a different class from that just mentioned, are found the manifestations of what has been called the "scrap pile of the Astral," and, indeed, that term of the workshop very aptly expresses it. On this sub-plane are to be found the discarded Astral materials of the Astral Bodies which have been "sloughed off" by entities which have discarded them as they have moved up higher. Also, the disintegrating Astral bodies of entities which have failed to survive and whose souls have been resolved into their original elements and become merged into the general principle of Consciousness, as described in a previous lesson. Remember, please, that these remnants of the Astral bodies so discarded and disintegrating, are not in any way related to the souls which formerly inhabited them. They are mere shells, *without soul or mind,* and yet preserving a slight degree of vitality, or "Vril." They are astral *corpses,* just as much a corpse as is the discarded physical body. But, just as the physical corpse may be aroused into apparent life activity by a strong galvanic current, and will roll its eyes, move its limbs, and even utter groans—so may these astral corpses be "galvanized" by the "Vril" of a medium (unconsciously by the latter), if the conditions be favorable, and may be materialized so as to appear as a shadowy form, acting, moving and even speaking, the only *mind* in it, however, being supplied by that of the medium or the persons present at the seance. These astral corpses also become visible under certain conditions, often around graveyards, battle-fields, etc., and are thought to be ghosts, or "spirits" of those who formerly inhabited them. They are, however, generally but the grossest astral covering of the Astral body—its "shell" so to speak, and are no more to be regarded as the deceased person himself than is the physical body lying in the grave—both are discarded coverings, or "corpses."

A psychic who, by means of untrained or misdirected psychic development, happens to wander on to this plane of the Astral, experiences a most unpleasant sight. It is not pleasant to roam in this charnel house of the Astral—this tomb of the Earth. An old Egyptian sage thus recorded his impressions of it: "What manner of place is this I see. It hath no water. It hath no air. It hath no light. It hath no foundation. It is unfathomably deep. It is as black as the blackest night." A modern investigator has said of this region—this Golgotha of the Astral: "Most students find the investigation of this section an extremely unpleasant task, for there appears to be a sense of density and gross materiality about it which is indescribably loathsome to the liberated Astral Body, causing the sense of pushing its way through some black viscous fluid, while the inhabitants and influences encountered there are unusually undesirable."

"And are there inhabitants of such a place?" one naturally asks. Alas, yes! There *are* denizens of this loathsome place—inhabitants of this horrible abode. Entities, however, not placed there for *punishment,* for no Being would entail such a fate upon the meanest and most depraved—or invent such a Hell. They are there because of their own abnormal desires and tendencies, which unfit them for the planes of even the lowest of disembodied human entities, and which also render them unfit for association with the disembodied astral forms of the beasts, which latter persist for a short time after physical death. "Then, what manner of creatures must these be?" you ask. "Fit for neither man nor beasts. Were they *human?*" And, one is forced to answer, "Yes!" Subject to the laws of humankind they are not allowed the privilege of rapid annihilation bestowed upon the beasts—they must live out their peculiar life to the end. They are the pariahs, the ghoul-like scum of the human race, who have removed themselves from the race fate and have entailed upon themselves a fate of their own. Their fate is a Living Death—a conscious life in a corpse-like body, among corpses of the Astral. These creatures are the disembodied entities of those who degenerated along abnormal sex lines—who attempted to reverse the Cosmic Law of Sex Polarity, and thus brought upon themselves the Recoil of the Life Forces. They were the lowest of the human Satyrs. Nature finally casts over them the spell of a deep sleep, from which they never awaken, and from which they pass into disintegration and annihilation. They polluted the Sacred Altar. They stole the Divine Fire for devilish rites. They committed the Unpardonable Sin. They removed themselves from the trend of Cosmic Evolution. Their own Desire was their Fate. We wish it were possible to speak plainer—but the time has not yet come.

LESSON XIV.
ASTRAL "BLACK-KEYS."

Before passing on to the sub-planes higher in degree and scale, let us call your attention to some of the minor sub-planes—the "black-keys" of the Astral scale. On these sub-planes dwell the nonhuman, or semi-human creatures which are grouped together in the occult classification under the general name of "elementaries" or "elementals." It is impossible for us to enter into a detailed consideration of this class of entities in a work of this general nature intended for popular reading. The reasons therefor would involve explanations which would crowd out of the space intended for them certain other details of the Astral Planes, and would even then be most incomplete and unsatisfying. Enough to say that occultists know that this planet, the earth, is the field and theatre for *three* distinct processes of evolution—that of the world that we know, human, animal, and vegetable; and two others of a different order. These two other fields of evolution have their own planes which are totally unrelated to ours. But these other evolutionary processes, although distinct from ours, nevertheless blend slightly with certain sub-planes of our Astral Planes—that is, the "edges overlap," if such a clumsy term may be used. Consequently, on certain of the "black-key" planes of our Astral, there may be found elementaries of a scale of life different from our own. This is but a general statement, the faults of which will be obvious to every advanced occultist who reads it—and yet such advanced student will see the necessity for the purposely imperfect statement in this place. Those who have read Bulwer's occult stories—notably "Zanoni," will recognize the nature of the entities of which we speak.

While the Arcane Teaching includes within its store of knowledge and information full details regarding these particular sub-planes which we have designated as the "black-keys" on the scale of the Astral Plane, and its Initiates who have attained certain degrees are fully informed regarding the same, still we are unable to make public at this time, place, and through this particular channel, the inner Arcane Teaching regarding the same. Personally, we think the time is ripe for such information to be plainly stated, accompanied by the necessary warnings; but those higher in authority among the Custodians have said to us: "Nay! Wait in patience! When the propitious hour is indicated by the planetary symbols—then may you open the sealed volume to those who would ree its riddles! For the present, the vow of silence maintains!" So there is naught left for us but to bow to the superior authority in the matter.

However, while we are not permitted to state the inner Arcane Teaching in this particular detail, the prohibition does not extend to our using quotations from other authorities who have already reported concerning these sub-planes of the Astral. And, believing that the said reports would be interesting to those of our students who take a scientific interest in this phase of occultism, we have decided to give you, in this lesson, very liberal quotations from a leading authority of another school of occultism, who has paid much attention to the phenomena of certain phases and planes of the Astral Plane, both in the direction of studying older and more advanced authorities, and also in the direction of personal investigation and exploration of these sub-planes, of the Astral. The latter is a task surrounded with dangers and risks which but few even advanced occultists care to undertake, and although we doubt the wisdom of the task, nevertheless we must admire the scientific ardor of the investigator.

The remainder of this lesson, indicated by quotation marks, consists of quotations from the said authority, investigator and explorer of these dark regions of the "black-keys" of the Astral.

The elementaries may be grouped into several general classes, although the classification is more or less unsatisfactory and imperfect, at the best. One of these classes comprise the entities which some writers have called "Nature Spirits," which term, however, is less accurate than poetical. These entities have been known in the legends by various names, prominent among which are the following: Earth-spirits, or gnomes; water-spirits, or undines; air-spirits, or sylphs; fire-spirits, or salamanders; fairies; pixies; elves; brownies; peris; djinns; trolls; fauns; kobolds; imps; goblins; little people; good people, etc., etc., of which the aforesaid authority says:

"Their forms are many and various, but most frequently human in shape, and somewhat diminutive in size. Like almost all inhabitants of the astral plane, they are able to assume any appearance at will, but they undoubtedly have definite forms of their own, or perhaps we should rather say favorite forms, which they wear when they have no special object in taking any other. Under ordinary conditions they are not visible to physical sight at all, but they have the power of making themselves so by materialization when they wish to be seen. There are an immense number of subdivisions or races among them, and individuals of these subdivisions differ in intelligence and disposition precisely as human beings do. The great majority of them apparently prefer to avoid man altogether; his habits and emanations are distasteful to them, and the constant rush of astral currents set up by his restless, ill-regulated desires, disturbs and annoys them. On the other hand, instances are not wanting in which nature-spirits have as it were made friends with human beings, and offered them such assistance as lay in their power, as in the well-known stories of the Scotch brownies or of the fire-lighting fairies.

This helpful attitude, however, is comparatively rare, and in most cases when they come in contact with man they either show indifference or dislike, or else take an impish delight in deceiving him and playing childish tricks upon him. Many a story illustrative of this curious characteristic may be found among the village gossip of the peasantry in almost any lonely mountainous district; and anyone who has been in the habit of attending *seances* for physical phenomena will recollect instances of practical joking and silly though usually good natured horse play, which almost always indicates the presence of some of these lower orders of astral spirits.

"The life periods of the different subdivisions vary greatly, some being quite short, others much longer than our human lifetime. We stand so completely outside such a life as theirs that it is impossible for us to understand much about its conditions; but it appears on the whole to be a simple, joyous, irresponsible kind of existence, much such as a party of happy children might lead among exceptionally physical surroundings. Though tricky and mischievous, they are rarely malicious unless provoked by some unwarrantable intrusion or annoyance; but as a body they also partake to some extent of the universal feeling of distrust for man, and they generally seem inclined to resent somewhat the first appearance of a neophyte on the astral plane, so that he usually makes their acquaintance under some unpleasant or terrifying form. If, however, he declines to be frightened by any of their freaks, they soon accept him as a necessary evil and take no further notice of him, while some among them may even after a time become friendly and manifest pleasure on meeting him.

"The Adept knows how to make use of the services of the nature spirits when he requires them, but the ordinary magician can obtain their assistance only by processes either of invocation or evocation; that is, either by attracting their attention as a suppliant and making some kind of bargain with them, or by endeavoring to set into motion influences which would compel their obedience. Both methods are extremely undesirable, and the latter is also excessively dangerous, as the operator would arouse a determined hostility which might prove fatal to him. Needless to say, no one studying occultism under a qualified Master would ever be permitted to attempt anything of the kind at all."

On other low planes of the Astral there is another class of elementaries, which have been called "artificial or man-created entities," of which the aforesaid authority says:

"This, the largest class of Astral entities, is also much the most important to man. Being entirely his own creation, it is inter-related with him by the closest bonds, and its action upon him is direct and incessant. It is an enormous inchoate mass of semi-intelligent entities, differing among themselves as human thoughts differ, and practically incapable of anything like classification and arrangement. The only division which can be usefully made is that which distinguishes between the artificial elementals made by the majority of mankind unconsciously, and those made by magicians with definite intent; while we may relegate to a third class the very small number of artificially arranged entities which are not elementals at all.

"The elemental essence which surrounds us on every side is in all its numberless varieties singularly susceptible to the influence of human thought. The action of the mere casual wandering thought upon it, causing it to burst into a cloud of rapidly-moving evanescent forms, has already been described; we have now to note how it is affected when the human mind formulates a definite, purposeful thought or wish. The effect produced is of the most striking nature. The thought seizes upon the plastic essence, and moulds it instantly into a living being of an appropriate form—a being which when once thus created is in no way under the control of its creator, but lives out a life of its own, the length of which is proportionate to the intensity of the thoughts or wish which called it into existence. It lasts in fact just as long as the thought-force holds it together. Most persons' thoughts are so fleeting that the elementals created by them last only a few minutes or a few hours, but an often-repeated thought or an earnest wish will form an elemental whose existence may extend to many days. Since the ordinary man's thoughts refer very largely to himself, the elementals which they form remain hovering about, and constantly tend to provoke a repetition of the idea which they represent, since such repetitions, instead of forming new elementals, would strengthen the old one, and give it a fresh lease of life. A man, therefore, who frequently dwells upon one wish often forms for himself an astral attendant which, constantly fed by fresh thought, may haunt him for years, ever gaining more and more strength and influence over Him; and it will easily be seen that if the desire be an evil one the effect upon his moral nature may be of the most disastrous character.

"Still more pregnant for good or evil are a man's thoughts about other people, for in that case they hover not about the thinker, but about the object of the thought. A kindly thought about any person, or an earnest wish for his good, will form and project towards him a friendly artificial elemental. If the wish be a definite one, as, for example, that he may recover from some sickness, then the elemental will be a force ever hovering over him to promote his recovery, or to ward off any influence that might tend to hinder it. In doing this it will display what appears like a very considerable amount of intelligence and adaptability, though really it is simply a force acting along the line of least resistance—pressing steadily in one direction all the time, and taking advantage of any channel that it can find, just as the water in a cistern would in a moment find the one open pipe among a dozen closed ones, and proceed to empty itself through that. If the wish be merely an indefinite one for his general good, the elemental essence in its wonderful plasticity will respond exactly to that less distinct idea also, and the creature formed will expend its force in the direction of whatever action for the man's advantage comes most readily to hand. In all cases, the amount of such force which it has to expend, and the length of time that it will live to expend it, depend entirely upon the strength of the original wish or thought which gave it birth; though it must be remembered that it can be, as it were, fed and strengthened, and its life-period protracted by other good wishes or friendly thoughts projected in the same direction. Furthermore, it appears to be actuated, like most other beings, by an instinctive desire to prolong its life, and thus reacts on its creator as a force constantly tending to provoke the renewal of the feelings which called it into existence. It also influences in a similar manner others with whom it comes into contact, though its *rapport* with them is naturally not so perfect.

"All that has been said as to the effect of good wishes and friendly thoughts is also true in the opposite direction of evil wishes and angry thoughts; and considering the amount of envy, hatred, malice and uncharitableness that exists in the world, it will be readily understood that among the artificial elemental many terrible creatures are to be seen. A man whose thoughts or desires are spiteful, brutal, sensual, avaricious, moves through the world carrying with him everywhere a pestiferous atmosphere of his own, peopled with the loathsome beings which he has created to be his companions. Thus he is not only in sadly evil case himself, but is a dangerous nuisance to his fellow-men, subjecting all who have the misfortune to come in contact with him to the risk of moral contagion from the influence of the abominations with which he chooses to surround himself.

"It occasionally happens, however, that an artificial elemental of this description is for various reasons unable to expend its force either upon its object or its creator, and in such cases it becomes a kind of wandering demon, readily attracted by any person who indulges feelings similar to that which gave it birth, and equally prepared either to stimulate such feelings in him for the sake of the strength it may gain from them, or to pour out its store of evil influences upon him through any opening which he may offer it. If it is sufficiently powerful to seize upon some passing shell (discarded astral body) it frequently does so, as the possession of such a temporary home enables it to husband its dreadful resources more carefully. In this form it may manifest through a medium, and by masquerading as some well-known friend may sometimes obtain an influence over people upon whom it would otherwise have little hold. ... Many a well-meaning man, who is scrupulously careful to do his duty toward his neighbor in word and deed, is apt to consider that his thoughts at least are nobody's business but his own, and so lets them run riot in various directions, utterly unconscious of the swarms of baleful creatures which he is launching upon the world. To such a man an accurate comprehension of the effect of thought and desire in producing artificial elementals would come as a horrifying revelation.

"Since such results as have been described above have been achieved by the thought-force of men who were entirely in the dark as to what they were doing, it will readily be imagined that a magician who understands the subject, and can see exactly what effect he is producing, may wield immense power along these lines. As a matter of fact, occultists of both the white and dark schools frequently use artificial elementals in their work, and few tasks are beyond the powers of such creatures when scientifically prepared and directed with knowledge and skill; for one who knows how to do so can maintain a connection with his elemental and guide it, no matter at what distance it may be working, so that it will practically act as though endowed with the full intelligence of its master.

"By some of the more advanced processes of Black Magic, also, artificial elementals of great power may be called into existence, and much evil has been worked in various ways by such entities. But it is true of them, as of the previous class, that if they are aimed at a person whom by reason of his purity of character they are unable to influence, they react with terrible force upon their creator; so that the mediaeval story of the magician being torn to pieces by the fiends he himself had raised, is no mere fable, but may well have had an awful foundation in fact.

Such creatures occasionally, for various reasons, escape from the control of those who are trying to make use of them, and become wandering and aimless demons, as do some of those mentioned under the previous heading under similar circumstances; but those that we are considering, having much more intelligence and power, and a much longer existence, are proportionately more dangerous. They invariably seek for means of prolonging their life, either by feeding like vampires upon the vitality of human beings, or by influencing them to make offerings to them; and among simple half savage tribes they have frequently succeeded in getting themselves recognized as village or family gods. ... By the vitality they draw from their devotees, they may continue to prolong their existence for many years, or even centuries, retaining sufficient strength to perform occasional phenomena of a mild type in order to stimulate the faith and zeal of their followers."

While the above quoted authority has placed what we consider to be undue emphasis upon the power of the elementals—for the human Will is sufficient to overcome their power, and they are prevented from coming to the mental atmosphere of all who do not attract them by virtue of the character of their own mental vibrations—nevertheless, we have thought it advisable to give you the benefit of this investigator's reports, for the purpose of warning you against dabbling in Evocations, and certain so called "magical" methods and practices. Black Magic in all of its forms result only in pain and evil to those indulging in them. He who invades planes of life foreign to his own, takes upon himself the risks inherent on such planes.

LESSON XV.
HIGHER ASTRAL PLANES.

We have now reached the point where we are called upon to consider the phases of the Astral Plane concerned with the state or condition of the disembodied entities of human beings. We call these the *higher* Astral Planes, only by way of contrast with the lower planes mentioned in the preceding two lessons, for some of these "higher" planes are quite low indeed as compared with the highest Astral Planes. Let us begin with the consideration of the lowest of these higher planes of the Astral, and then proceed to consider the planes higher in the scale.

In the first place, we must remember that the disembodied human soul leaves the physical in a state or condition akin to sleep. It is carried by the attraction of its nature and character to the highest plane consistent with its nature—that is, to a plane corresponding with the highest qualities existent within itself. And upon that plane it gradually awakens into the Astral life of that particular plane. The conditions of the Astral Life are so different from that of the Material Plane that it is difficult to intelligently describe it in terms of the latter. For instance, the souls on the higher planes are able to enter into conscious relationship with those on the lower planes, but those on the lower planes cannot enter into conscious relationship with those on the higher planes except through the act of those dwelling on the higher. Each plane has planes higher and lower than itself, the above law being operative in all cases. The higher plane souls have access to the lower, but the lower may not invade the higher. And this *access* is not in the nature of a *physical visit* from the higher to the lower, but is in the nature of a psychic consciousness, akin to Clairvoyance, in which the soul, while remaining on its own plane, still seems to have traveled to the others, there to converse with other souls on these planes. The soul itself, unless very advanced, does not realize the nature of the connection but thinks that it actually *travels* to the scene of the lower planes. The analogy of Clairvoyance on the Material Plane will give you the idea of the process.

When a soul awakens on its own plane of the Astral, it finds it difficult to realize that it is not alive in the flesh, and often much time is required before it realizes its true condition. Then it begins to manifest an interest in its surroundings, and pays many visits on its own and other planes (in the manner before mentioned) renewing old acquaintances and relationships, and manifesting the activities quite natural for a human being under such circumstances. But sooner or later this life begins to pall upon it, and it passes into the Idealistic State, which we shall describe a little further on. Enough for the moment to say that in the Idealistic State the soul begins to manifest its ideals—the things it has hoped for, dreamed of, and longed for in its earth life. The greater the idealistic quality of the soul, the greater the extent and range of its Idealistic State. But before considering this interesting phase of Astral Life, let us see what happens on the lower planes, to those who have but few ideals, and those of a most material nature.

On the very lowest of these planes of the Astral we find the "earth bound" entities, or souls, of many degrees. These are the souls of those who are so material in their tastes, habits and trend of thought and desire that they can never rise to the higher states and conditions of the Astral. They stay close to the earth, mingling unseen in the scenes which they so loved during their life in the body, and yet being unable to actually participate in the carnal manifestations, unless, indeed, some particularly attractive dweller in the flesh opens his physical organism to the obsession of some affinitive and congenial companion of the lower Astral Planes and allows the entity to manifest through his physical body. These entities are found in great numbers in the astral atmosphere of low resorts, and similar places, where they poison the psychic atmosphere to such an extent that their presence may be *felt,* and often *seen* by sensitive persons who happen to visit such places.

We may add as a caution to those who are fond of dabbling in the psychic process of Evocation, that it is largely from this class of entities that many of the "spirits" appearing at *seances* are drawn. It is this class of entities who so often impersonate your disembodied friends and relatives, and whose sneers and ribaldry are scarcely concealed behind the loving messages and "spirit wisdom" which they pass on to the wondering mortal in the flesh who would not dream of associating with their kind in earth life.

The life of these entities on the Astral Plane is not long. They find but little pleasure, and much torment, in life apart from the physical, for their desires are altogether along physical lines. They are filled with dissatisfaction, *ennui,* and weariness. As a writer has said: "The disembodied learn that the Hades of Immortality is the lack of a physical body." Their dissatisfaction soon sets into operation the *desire to be relieved of the burden,* and the "Will-not-to Live" manifests itself. They drop into a dream state, or somnambulistic condition, in which they *dream out* their desires and tastes to the end—until they have exhausted every mental longing within their nature. There being nothing left of them, when these mental states have been lived out, they weaken and pass into unconsciousness, which is followed by death on the Astral with consequent disintegration and annihilation as entities. Their dream state is, in a way, their Idealistic State—all the Idealistic State they are capable of, at any rate. This is not in any way a *punishment*—merely a natural consequent of their nature. As the old saying goes:

"One cannot make a silk-purse out of a sow's ear." Nor can one get more than a pint out of a pint measure. *Desire* is the cause of their life, and of their death. Balance is manifested and preserved. Water cannot rise above the level of its own source. These entities receive "their own," as much as do those on the higher planes. There is no injustice manifested here.

Rising in the scale we find souls who while attached to material things nevertheless have had *ideals* during their life—things for which they had hoped, and dreamt, prayed and longed. As the scale advances we find that the nature of the ideals advance from lower to higher—but the principle is the same. And for the lowest to the highest of these ideal degrees, the Astral Life contains that peculiar and wonderful condition or state known as the "Idealistic State." And this Idealistic State is the real Astral Life of the soul, into which it enters after it has tired of the conditions it finds at first on the Astral Plane. It is composed of a condition or state, or series of such conditions or states, in which it *lives out in vivid imagination, or realistic dream-like states all of its unrealized personal ideals, hopes, expectations, desires, ambitions, aspirations, longings, and inclinations of its nature.*

It may be objected to that this is but a state of illusion or delusion, and not a reality. But it must be remembered that even on the Material Plane: *"Dreams are true while they last!"* On the Astral Plane, in the Idealistic State, these dreams exceed in vividness and reality anything that the embodied mortal ever experiences. So far as the soul is concerned the experiences through which it lives in the Idealistic State are just as *real* as anything that it ever experienced in physical life. Every element of reality is there. And there *is a* reality about it that all advanced occultists recognize. At the last, one's experiences in physical life may be resolved to a "series of mental states"—and what less than this does the Astral dreamer experience? And what more than a Dream, after all is the experience of the earth-life of three-score-and-ten of the average person? "Like dreams they come, like dreams they go." In its way, and on its plane, the Idealistic State is just as *real* as the physical life.

In this Idealistic State, the dreaming soul lives out countless lives, of infinite variety. Just as in an ordinary dream, Time is annihilated and one may live out a lifetime in the space of a second, so in the Idealistic State the soul lives out centuries of experiences in a moment To all intents and purposes, the soul—every soul in fact—lives an Eternity in the Idealistic State, although the entire experience may occur in a few years (as *we* know time). Time is measured only by "happenings," and the happenings of an Eternity may be crowded into a very short space of ordinary time, in the Idealistic State. Every possibility within its personality is lived out, outlived, and exhausted in interest, in the Idealistic State. Just as in the moment of physical death, the soul sees as in a flash its entire earth-life in one great panorama—past and present being at once—so in the Idealistic State the soul lives out every personal desire, aim, aspiration, hope, ambition, longing, and wish, in an infinite series of states or lives. *It realizes every personal ideal* inherent within it, to the utmost. Its fullest personal Heart's Desire is attained. There is no unsatisfied personal longing, or unrealized ideal, left at the end of the Idealistic State of the soul on the Astral Plane. Think what this means, please. Think what it must mean to live out to the full "The Might Have Been," which is in the life of every human being. Think what it must mean to manifest one's love to the utmost—to have every wish granted—every ambition satisfied. Think what it must be to live out one's life *as one wishes it had been lived*—with all the mistakes corrected, all the errors remedied, all the problems solved, all the atonements made, all the injustices rectified. The Idealistic State is the living over of your life As You Wish It Could Have Been. Nay, more, living it over countless times, each variation bringing out some new point and feature of unrealized ideals, desires, and wishes! It is a state in which the verse of Kipling comes true:

> "And only the Master shall praise us,
> And only the Master shall blame;
> And no one shall work for money,
> And no one shall work for fame;
> But each for the joy of the working,
> And each in his separate star,
> Shall draw the Thing as he sees it
> For the God of Things as They are!"

But it is only a *dream,* you say. Nay, more than a dream as you understand the term. A dream it is, but a dream so *real* that naught but Omniscience could distinguish the difference. A dream so *real* that it equals the thing that we call Life, in every element of reality. In the end, one is as Real as the other—Earth Life and the Astral Idealistic State. And, also, in the end, one is as Unreal as the other.

But not only are the high personal desires, aspirations and ideals so lived out in the Idealistic State. The low personal desires, aspirations and ideals are also passed through this threshing-mill of the Idealistic State. One lives out to the utmost, in some of the series of these dream-lives, *all* the possibilities of his nature or character—good and bad alike. In fact, the lowest desires and ideals are the first to manifest, and the first to die out and be lived out. To those who have no others, the end then comes. But to those who have higher ideals and desires mingled with the lower, there then comes a stage of living out the higher part of their nature. And as time passes, the soul rises far above all the dross and grossness of its nature, and lives in the higher regions of itself—enjoying to the fullest the satisfaction which comes only from those higher states. But, the soul must *possess* the higher in order to manifest it. Unless the higher be involved within the soul, it cannot be evolved. What does not exist cannot be manifested.

While in this Idealistic State, the soul may be attracted by those on earth who are related to it by the old ties or affection or interest, and in such case it may manifest by communications. But these communications can contain *only that which the soul knows and experiences at the time.* It merely reports what it is experiencing—merely its own personal experiences of the Idealistic State. And even this it reports in a dazed, dreamy fashion. Thus the devout Christian soul will report that it is dwelling in a Heaven of orthodox surroundings—the golden streets, harps, and milk and honey being described in detail. A good Catholic soul will report a Catholic Heaven, with all the saints present; while a good Baptist soul will report a Heaven along strictly Baptist lines—close communion, and only immersed souls being in evidence. A Moslem will describe himself as enjoying all the delights of the Heaven promised by Mohammed. And the soul of the Unbeliever will inform you that "there is nothing in this Heaven business at all"; and that the "after life" is merely a life among congenial companions, thinking along the same lines as himself; and that he is of the opinion that the church people have perished, instead of having gained immortality. And so on, each "painting the Thing as he sees it" as the world of "Things as They Are." And each is telling the Truth, as he sees it, from his own viewpoint. Strange, but true!

Those who complain of the absence of the qualities of Heaven and Hell in this Idealistic State have not thought deeply enough regarding it. In the attainment of the highest ideals and aspirations, there is contained all that men have pictured as the joys of Heaven—*and infinitely more.* And in the living out of the consequences of evil desire and low ideals, and all that goes with this state, there is all that the most fervent Calvinist could wish for in a Hell—*and infinitely more.*

But, remember always, that the Heaven and Hell of the Idealistic State is not a punishment or reward bestowed for good or evil deeds—it is but the working out of Cause and Effect—the fullest manifestation of Desire and one's Character. And, in the adjustment acts restrained by Fear equal Acts performed. "As a man thinketh in his heart, so is he" in the Idealistic State. In the working out of Cause and Effect in the Idealistic State of the Astral, it is indeed true that: "He who hates is an assassin; he who covets is a thief; he who lusts is an adulterer; that the gist of a crime is the desire behind it." This Idealistic State of the Astral Plane is not Fate, not Providence, not Destiny, not Reward and Punishment—it is but the operation of natural laws of Cause and Effect, Orderly Trend, and Logical Sequence, on the Astral Plane. "From one, know All."

And, in the working out of the Idealistic State of the Astral, the most unpleasant experiences are lived through first, and then the higher ideals begin to manifest themselves—the soul rising to higher and still higher flights, until at last it reaches the highest degree possible to it by reason of its constitution, nature and character. And in that Life, if it be prepared to receive it, it may receive instruction from Beings higher in the scale, as well as from the more evolved souls of our own race who are attracted to it by reason of its desires and ideals. Many a soul has received the help which led it to Individuality, in this Idealistic State. Many an Individual soul has so received instruction which led to better conditions for growth in the next incarnation. "When the pupil is ready, the Master appears" on the Astral Plane as on the Material Plane. If you possess the seed of the ideal, the blossom and the fruit will surely be yours.

When the impulses arising from the personal desires, aspirations, and ideals of the soul have expended themselves fully, and the "personality" of the soul has been "lived out and outlived" in the process—when there remain no further impulses of personality to exert themselves in the Idealistic State—then the soul finds that it "has nothing more to live for" along the lines of personality. It feels aged, tired and weary, and the desire for *rest* creeps over it, and it gradually sinks into a dreamless sleep, which ends in the Death of the Personality. If Egohood has *not* been attained by the soul, then it never awakens into a new life, for Personality being all that it possesses, and all personality being expended and exhausted, then there is nothing left to persist in new birth. But if Egohood has been attained, and the soul realizes that it is more than the "Me" of itself, then when the "Me" dies away, the "I" finds itself still existent and filled with the impulse of the Will-to-Live of the Cosmic Will, which urges it forward to re-birth in new bodies, to seek further and more advanced experience. Even in this case the soul falls into the deep Astral sleep, but awakens therefrom when it is reborn into a new body, under circumstances and environments in accordance with the Law of Attraction resulting from the *essence of the past life,* the latter inhering to it. The Ego then will be free from its lived-out desires and will no longer be hampered by them. It will be attracted toward new scenes and fields of activity. In its new body it will have to combat the inherited impulses and desires of its new

"Me," but it will always feel its superiority to the latter, and will feel the ability to *stand aside and look at its personality*.

The advanced Ego, in time, reaches the stage of *conscious* re-birth, in which the Ideal Life is *consciously continuous* with the old life, and which is *consciously* followed by the new birth. We have spoken of these things in our lesson on "Survival of the Fittest" which you should now re-read in the light of the present lesson.

There are many planes of the Astral much higher than even these which we have described, but a description of them would be impossible except to highly advanced occultists. Some of these higher Astral Planes transcend the imagination of the average person leading the personal life today, on earth. And yet, over and above the entire Astral Plane, there is the great Spiritual Plane, which we would lack words to even faintly designate. And yet, even these exalted Planes await your coming, O Neophyte, whose feet are now well set upon The Path!

PART VI. OCCULT FORCES.

Lesson XVI. Psychic Phenomena.

Lesson XVII. Mentalism.

Lesson XVIII. Invocation and Evocation.

The Arcane Teaching

LESSON XVI.
PSYCHIC PHENOMENA.

For the sake of convenience in considering the various phases of the phenomena of the Occult Forces operative in the Cosmos, we have divided the same into three general classes, as follows: (1) Psychic Phenomena, consisting of the manifestation of the phases generally known as Clairvoyance, Clairaudience, Psychometry, Telepathy, etc., the distinguishing feature of which is the "knowing" of events other than through the ordinary senses; (2) Mentalism, consisting of the manifestations of Mental Influence, Mind-Power, Thought-Force, Mental Magic, etc., the distinguishing feature of which is the exerting of the influence of one mind over other minds; (3) Invocation and Evocation, consisting of the "calling upon" supernatural beings, or the "calling forth" of disembodied entities; elementals; vitalized thought-entities, etc., from the Astral Plane.

These manifestations, and the force which produces them have been called "Occult" because of the fact that they belong to the less understood phases of natural forces and phenomena. The word "Occult" means: "secret or hidden from the eye or understanding; not seen or understood; mysterious, invisible, unknown, undetected, etc." To many persons, Occultism is considered to be concerned with supernatural forces, things, and manifestations. This is erroneous, for there is nothing *super*-natural—nothing outside of or over nature, of which we can ever have any knowledge. Every thing in the Cosmos is *natural,* and under natural laws. The Law is the only *super*-natural that there is or can be—and we can know It only as being in actual existence; we can know nothing of its inner nature, for it is not a "thing" with attributes, qualities or limitations, as we understand those terms. Everything in the Cosmos is *natural*—the unknown as well as the commonly known. Therefore, when we say "occult" we mean merely some natural thing, force, or manifestation, not commonly known or recognized by men. When a thing, force, or manifestation becomes commonly known, it ceases to be regarded as "occult." Electricity was once regarded as an "occult" force—but today it is commonly known and employed, although its real nature is still a mystery. To the trained and advanced Occultist the so-called Occult Forces are just as familiar and *natural* as are the manifestations of force common to the knowledge of the race. The Occult Forces are simply finer forces of nature, which are not recognized, known or understood by the average person of the race, today. We wish this to be thoroughly understood. There are no supernatural forces, things, or manifestations—all are natural, and under natural laws.

Let us now proceed to a consideration of the class of occult phenomena which we have grouped under the sub-title, "Psychic Phenomena," and which are known severally as Clairvoyance, Clairaudience, Psychometry, Telepathy, etc., the distinguishing feature of which is the "knowing" of events through other channels than the ordinary senses. These several phases are but modifications of one general phenomenon—Astral Sensing.

The majority of modern writers upon the subject of Psychic Phenomena lay great stress upon the "vibrations, waves, currents, etc.," by which psychic impressions are transmitted from one mind to another, or by which one "senses" occurrences in points of space far removed from him. We have no objection to these terms, for they represent the best available words to describe the actual details of the manifestation—but these words must be used understandingly. The idea, so commonly advanced, that these "vibrations" or "waves" or "currents" are but forms of *etheric* vibrations similar in nature to the waves of light, heat, electricity, material magnetism, etc., is erroneous, and gives a materialistic tinge to phenomena which are of a much higher plane than that of material forces and substance. While there is a general resemblance between all planes of the Manifest Cosmos, owing to the Law of Analogy which causes "correspondences" on all planes—"as above, so below"—and "from one know all"—still the vibrations, waves and currents concerned in Psychic Phenomena and Mentalism belong to an entirely different plane from that of those concerned in the manifestation of light, heat, electricity, etc., which belong to lower planes.

In the preceding lessons, we have shown you that there are three Principles manifesting and active in Cosmos, viz., Substance, Motion, and Consciousness. In each of these three Principles, there are manifested correspondences which we may call "vibrations," "waves," "currents," etc. On the plane of Substance, we have vibrations and waves of matter, which result in the various forms, shapes, and action of material objects. This is caused by the Principle of Motion acting upon the Principle of Substance. Much that we call energy or force is but the appearance of fine degrees of Substance energized by Motion. Electricity, for instance, is but a fine form of Substance, so energized. The Ether, itself, is but a fine form of Substance, almost approaching Pure Energy, but not passing over the line which divides Energy from Substance. There are also vibrations and waves of Pure Motion, which may be considered, mentally, as independent of Substance, although we can never know them as such. There is a plane of Pure Motion, which is unthinkable except to minds which have been trained to grasp the subject. And, likewise, there are vibrations, waves, and currents in the *Principle of Consciousness,* produced by the action of Motion upon that Principle. And it is to this plane that the "vibrations, waves, and currents" concerned with Psychic Phenomena properly belong. They are *not* "waves in the Ether," for the Ether is on the material plane. They are "waves in the Mind Principle" itself, which is quite another thing.

Without attempting to lead you into an extended discussion of the scientific details of the matter, we would call your attention to his one fact which should serve to give you a plain mental picture of the phenomenon—a general outline of a picture, into which you can fill the details as you proceed in the study and experimental work along these lines. This general statement is as follows: The Cosmos is known to be practically a great World-Brain, in which Thoughts become Things, taking on Substantial Form. With a Cosmos *mental in nature*—consisting in fact of but One Universal Mind in which all particular things are but *Centres of Consciousness*—can you not see that there must be a Circulation of Consciousness, or Currents of Thought, just as there is a circulation of water in and by the currents of the ocean; or as there is a circulation of air by reason of the currents therein; or as there is a circulation of electricity, light, and all other forms of what we call Energy. *Consciousness is a Principle,* just as is Substance or Motion, and *what is true of one Principle is true of the other two,* according to the Law of Analogy. Therefore, there are Vibrations, Waves, and Currents of Consciousness, just as truly as there are corresponding manifestations on the material plane. And you may use these terms, very properly—always avoiding the mistake of confusing them with the material correspondences.

In Clairvoyance, Clairaudience, Psychometry, and Telepathy, we have several forms of manifestation of the existence of these Mental Waves and Currents, for so we shall call them to avoid the necessity of longer terms. But how does the mind of the person receive and register the impressions received through these Mental Currents? It is known to be a fact that no mind can receive impressions without the agency and medium of *some form of material organ,* though that material organ may be extremely subtle and fine. And this rule holds true in the case of the phenomena which we are now considering. And such organs *do* exist, and are called the Organs of Astral Sense. In the lessons treating of the Astral Plane, you have been informed of the existence of the Astral Body, the subtle counterpart of the Physical Body. This Astral Body is endowed with counterparts of the physical senses, which it may use in sensing the objects and impressions of the Astral Plane. In this way Astral Sensing becomes possible. The average person has not used these Astral Senses sufficiently well to develop them for active use, but this development is possible to those who have sufficient interest and patience to undertake the task. But here and there are found persons whose Astral Senses manifest their existence in a degree not known to the average person. These persons become very sensitive to the impressions of the Astral Plane, and although, as a rule, they are untrained and do not comprehend the nature of the phenomena, still they afford conclusive proof of the existence of the faculties in question. We shall not attempt to "prove" the existence of Psychic Phenomena in these lessons. We have not the space at our disposal, nor is it within the scope of this particular work. Evidence of such nature as to convince any unprejudiced persons may be found in many books on the subject, notably the reports of the English Society for Psychical Research. Moreover many persons have experienced these facts in their own lives.

Let us first consider the phenomenon generally called "Clairvoyance" which is defined as: "A faculty or power by which the clairvoyant is able to see mentally things concealed from sight; to see and describe things happening at a distance." With the exception of cases in which the person actually travels in his Astral Body to distant scenes, and there witnesses with his Astral Senses the events actually occurring there, all Clairvoyance results from one general cause, and in the same general way. Let us suppose an event occurring at a distant place. In the manifestation of that event there occurs a constant, regular and continuous series of conscious states on the part of all things concerned therein. Not only on the part of all living things is there consciousness manifested, but there is a consciousness manifested by all inanimate things present upon the scene—things inorganic as well as organic, in the usual use of these terms. As we have said on page 60 (Lesson IV): "Those who have studied along occult lines have become aware of the existence of mind and consciousness in so-called inanimate objects—the minerals, metals, etc., and even in the atoms—and finally in the Ether. Everything in the Manifest Cosmos has *some degree* of Consciousness." This being so, it follows that such Consciousness must follow the natural law, and transmit waves or currents—waves and currents of Consciousness—which travel and *circulate* on the Astral Plane where they may be sensed by those astral organs attuned to receive them. Just as the Marconigrams may be received only by instruments keyed to the proper degree of receptivity, so may these currents be received only by those who are in tune with them.

One whose Astral Senses are sufficiently sensitive, and attuned, may receive and register these currents, just as the physical eye registers the light waves of the ether, or the ear the sound waves of the air. There is not necessarily a projection of the Astral Body to the scene of the happening—the Astral Senses may register the impressions received from the currents of Consciousness. To those who may doubt the reasonableness of *sensing* things and events over thousands of miles, we would say that it is simply an Astral correspondence of the Physical phenomenon of Sight, whereby impressions are received from the distant stars, over billions of miles—over distances so vast that it requires centuries for the light waves to travel. And, remember this—the physical eye never actually sees the outer objects themselves, but merely sees the effects produced upon the nerves by the waves of light.

Nor does a person fail to see the outside object, but he also fails to see even the light-waves themselves—he merely *sees* certain vibrations of nerve-substance set up in the brain by the action of the light vibrations. And this is in every sense no less wonderful than the phenomena of Astral Sensing which we have just described—merely a little more common and familiar, that is all. If we had as full and common a development of the Astral Senses as we have of the physical, we would consider it no more remarkable to *see* events occurring in India, than to witness the changes on the planet Mars. One is as natural as the other, Clairaudience is but another phase of Astral Sensing, by which the Astral Senses receive the impression of sounds, instead of sights. The principle involved is the same.

So far we have spoken only of Clairvoyance in its phase of sensing distant objects. There are other phases, to the consideration of which we shall now pass. But before leaving this phase, we wish to put ourselves squarely on record regarding the nature of the majority of cases of genuine Clairvoyance. In spite of the opinions of many able authorities, we believe that the manifestation of the above form of Distant Clairvoyance is very rare and uncommon. We believe that but few persons ever experience it, even spontaneously. We believe that the majority of recorded cases of Distant Clairvoyance are instances either of Telepathy of a high order, or else of actual Astral Projection, which we believe to be far more common than is usually believed. We believe that a great number of cases of Clairvoyance are due to the unconscious projection of the Astral Body to the distant scene, if even but for a moment—for time is practically annihilated in Astral Projection.

Clairvoyance of Past Events, is explained by the Arcane Teachings as resulting from the fact that in the Cosmic Brain events leave their records and impression, just as the events of the experience of a man leave records and impressions in *his* brain. These recorded impressions constitute subconscious Memory, in the case of both the man's brain and the Cosmic Brain—"from one know all"—"as below, so above." On the Astral Plane there are preserved the records of the Cosmos—the Cosmic Subconscious Memory, in fact. Every thing, action, thought, deed, or activity of any kind, degree or description, that has been manifested since the Dawn of the Cosmic Day, is there recorded in the great unforgetting Subconscious Memory of the Cosmos. All occultists know this, and have called this Subconscious Memory Record by different names. Some minds, peculiarly attuned, occasionally enter into conscious relationship with this Cosmic Subconscious Memory, and are able to record, generally more or less imperfectly, what they sense there.

This may be done, either through psychic sensing of mental currents arising from these states of Subconscious Memory, or else by actual contact with them in the Astral Body. But, the phenomena is far less common than is generally supposed, and many cases are explainable upon the hypothesis of Telepathy—that is the impressions are thought impressions, either emanating from the mind of some person now living in the physical, or else some persistent thought-currents which have maintained their coherent properties over long periods of time.

Clairvoyance of the Future, is a misnomer. It implies actual existence somewhere of a foreknowledge or Foresight of the Future—which does not exist. If such existed, then Fate or Predestination would be true. The Cosmic Mind does not *know* before the manifestation—for the knowing causes the manifestation. But the phenomena which is known by the name of Clairvoyance of the future, *does* exist, although the theories concerning it are erroneous. It is true that occasionally individuals seem able to foretell with more or less accuracy, the events which afterward come true at least partially. The secret consists in the fact that the Laws of Orderly Trend and Sequence being operative, there must always be in existence the "shadows cast by the approaching events"—that is active causes operating in the direction of bringing about certain effects. Among these active causes, Desire and Mental Pictures in the minds of living human beings play an important part. The Clairvoyant perceiving the evidences of these active causes in the Astral is often able to make very good guesses or intuitive conjectures of the events which will follow. Just as one may predict something that will happen tomorrow, from something that is happening to-day. But there is no *certainty* about the prediction, in either case. For there may be, and generally are, other causes which will play their part at the time of action, and thus defeat the entire prediction. Clairvoyance of the Future perceives *probable effects of existent causes*— but no more. The Future is not in existence in the mind of any being— not even in the Mind of the Cosmos. Make no mistake about this. Even Astrology can indicate only "probabilities" of the future.

Psychometry, or the receiving of impressions from inanimate objects, by which one enters into *rapport* (or psychic connection) with the previous environment of the object—thus learning its previous history, particulars of its environment, etc., is explained by the fact that in the object's consciousness (for all objects possess a degree of consciousness) there is preserved a memory of its past environment, history, etc., which may be read by the mind attuned to the impressions. Not only this, but the object is still astrally connected by psychic filaments with its previous environment, and the Clairvoyant may thus enter into *rapport* with the latter and its stored-up memories. The object gives the Clairvoyant "the loose end" of the psychic ball of memory and association, which he then unwinds.

LESSON XVII.
MENTALISM.

Under the head of "Mentalism" we shall group that general class of occult phenomena which consists of the manifestations of what has been called Mental Influence, Mind Power, Thought Force, Mental Magic, Mental Suggestion, etc., the distinguishing feature of which is the exerting of the influence of one mind over other minds. This phase of occult phenomena is well known to the general public of to-day, by reason of the great interest which has been manifested in late years regarding the influence of the mind over physical states, and the investigations and literature which have resulted by reason thereof. But this power, and the knowledge thereof, is no new thing, by any means. We find traces of it in the history of every one of the ancient peoples, as well as in the records of the nations of comparatively modern times. The hierophants of ancient Egypt, Chaldea and Greece were adepts in all of the various branches of mentalism and understood the true underlying principles far better than do the majority of the teachers and writers upon the subject to-day. The traditions and legends coming to us from old Atlantis, inform us of the high degree of knowledge of these things were possessed by that wonderful people who inhabited what is now the "Lost Continent."

To understand Mentalism, one must understand the nature of Telepathy, or Transference of Thought. We hear much of Telepathy in these latter days in the many books and magazines devoted to the subject, in plays, and in the teachings of the various metaphysical cults which have sprung into prominence. Many are the theories advanced to account for the phenomena, and manifold is the error that has arisen from imperfect and incorrect statements of the underlying principles. On the one hand, we hear much of theories of "the ether waves" which carry the "thought vibrations," both being likened to, and held as, but higher forms, of the other vibrations of the ether. On the other hand, we hear many theories which seek to account for the phenomena on supernatural grounds—the desirable forms being considered the evidences of divine power, and the undesirable being regarded as arising from diabolical sources. But there is nothing supernatural about the matter, nor are the waves and vibrations "etheric." We have explained the matter in the preceding lesson, and have shown how the Circulation of Mind is sufficient to account for the phenomena.

That the Thought of man is an actual, moving force, is a fact well known to all occultists, ancient and modern. That thought waves travel in currents and waves is a fact not only believed because of the ancient teachings, but also because those who are able to sense on the Astral Plane are able to *see* the passage of these thought waves, and currents, as they pass from one mind to others. Not only is thought-force exerted consciously, and with direct intent, but also unconsciously and with direct intent and purpose on the part of the person who exerts it. Thought is as real a force as is electricity, although it operates on an entirely different plane. It may be compared to magnetism and electricity, because it is the correspondence of the physical fine forces, on the mental plane. But one must not make the mistake of supposing that these thought waves or currents, or other forms of influence, travel through the ether as do light, electricity and material magnetism. On the contrary, they have nothing to do with the ether as a medium. They travel through the Universal Principle of Mind.

We have seen, in preceding lessons, that the Three Cosmic Principles pervade all space—the Cosmos—and one of those Principles is Consciousness—Mind. Do you realize just what this means? That all the space there is, or can be—Infinite Space—is occupied by the Mind Principle of the Cosmos? That pervading all space there is a great Cosmic Ocean of Mind, living throbbing, pulsating with life and energy, in the depths of which there is the quietude of eternal calm and peace—on the surface of which are ripples, eddies, waves, currents and whirlpools—upon and in which there is manifested the phases of the fiercest tempest and of absolute calm, rest and peace. And in this great Ocean of Mind—in the Cosmic Mind Principle—occur all the multitude of manifestations of Consciousness that are known on the lower planes of life—on the human plane—and on the planes far beyond any possible conceptions of beings on the lowly scale of mankind of to-day?

The would-be authorities and instructors on the subject of Mentalism speak learnedly of the "etheric waves" by which Thought is carried from mind to mind. They do not dream, these founders of latter-day schools and cults, that for thousands of years the Arcane Teachers have known and taught that even this much vaunted Universal Ether in which is supposed to abide the foundation principles of all things—this Something which Science says is a No-Thing containing the infinite possibilities of Everything—is but the lowest of the scale of the *seven Ethers* known to the occultists, and which highest and lowest Ethers are but manifestations in the Cosmic Brain, *a result of Mind!* And to suppose that Mind needs this lowest Ether to convey its currents of mental energy is as much a folly and inversion of Truth as that conveyed in the materialistic dogmas that "mind is a secretion and by-product of Matter!" These pseudomentalists do not know the first principle of Mentalism, when they assert that Mental Currents are but higher forms of "etheric waves" and energy. In time, they will learn that the Ether is the byproduct of Mind, and rests in the Ocean of Mind just as the dissolved salt rests in the Ocean of Water. We do not say this in the spirit of captious criticism—that would be a waste of words and time—but because we realize that unless the fundamental Truth is comprehended and realized the study of Mentalism will be but a phase of the study of *physical* science, which it infinitely transcends in importance.

Mind requires Substance in order to manifest itself, *but it travels in its own medium.* Its waves are waves of Mind—its currents are currents of Mind—its vibrations are vibrations of Mind. Activities in a Centre of Consciousness are not confined to that particular centre of manifestation, but extend in all directions in rapidly widening circles, unless the sender deliberately concentrates his thought force in a special and particular direction, either by conscious intent, or else by reason of intense Desire. This Thought-force flows out in currents and waves, exerting more or less influence upon all minds with which it comes in contact, the degree depending upon the degree of harmony to the particular vibrations which are manifested in the receptive minds.

But all this is an old story to the majority of our readers. There is scarcely need for us to write regarding these fundamental facts of Mentalism. They have been told, and often very well told, by the many writers on the subject, who have discovered the facts of the operation of these mental forces, although often in ignorance of the fundamental principles involved in the phenomena. Every student of these lessons has read much regarding the operations of thought influence, and to repeat these familiar facts would be akin to repeating the instructions in kindergarten work, and the alphabet, to advanced students. We shall, therefore, take it for granted that the student is informed regarding these elementary facts in Mentalism, and shall now merely show how they are explained by the underlying principles of the Arcane Teaching. In our supplementary work, "The Arcane Formulas; or, Mental Alchemy," we shall give the formulas for the actual demonstration and manifestation of these principles. These lessons are not for beginners, but for those who have acquainted themselves with the reality of Mental Influence and Thought-Force, and who have passed the kindergarten stage of occult attainment and knowledge.

The existence of Mental Influence in its various phases has been fully established to the satisfaction of thousands of investigators. The facts of hypnotism are now common property. The existence of "absent treatments" and other phases of telepathic influence is now accepted as fact by the majority of students of the subject. What is known as "personal magnetism" is now understood to result from purely mental causes. The Attractive power of Thought—the Drawing Power of Mind—the operation of the great Law of Mental Attraction—these things are recognized by students of the subject, and hundreds of books have been written explaining (?) them under one hypothesis or another, and giving more or less valuable instructions in their use. We shall not dwell upon these details at this place—our little book "The Arcane Formulas; or, Mental Alchemy" will furnish the "how" side of this subject, in a condensed, plain, practical and "usable" form. What we wish to do now is to acquaint you with the real underlying principle of Mental Influence—the one fact which illumines the entire subject—which has been known to and taught by the Arcane Teachers for thousands of years, but which does not seem to be known to the latter-day teachers along these lines. We ask you to pay close attention to what we have to say on this point, for when you grasp this underlying principle you have the key to the whole range of phenomena.

The secret of Mental Influence—the effect of one mind over the other minds—lies in the fact that *there is sex in mind*. Under the Law of Opposites, in its phase of Sex Polarity, we find the interesting fact that there is to be found evidences of Sex Polarity on all planes of activity and in all forms of activity, inorganic as well as organic. Sex Polarity is manifested even by the atoms, in the attractions and repulsions. In electricity and magnetism the polarity manifested is all along the lines of Sex Polarity. (We explain this in our supplementary work entitled, "The Mystery of Sex; or, Sex Polarity.") And on the mental plane this principle is found in full operation. The manifestation of Will is the action of the Masculine Principle. Desire and Imagination are phases of the Feminine Principle. Thought, Reason and Intellectual activities result from the union of the two principles. Desire, the female principle of Mind, arouses and attracts the Will, the Masculine element, and draws it into action. Imagination, another phase of the feminine principle, acts in the same way. But, yet, the action of Will is the inciting cause of the activities of Desire and Imagination. The Will can *create* only by its action upon the feminine principles of Desire and Imagination—it cannot create by itself. On the other hand, the feminine principles of Desire and Imagination cannot produce and create without the union with the Will. This is merely the general outline of the activities.

But, and here is where the explanation of Mental Influence is seen, both the feminine Desire and the masculine Will of a person may be incited into activity by the Will or Desire, as the case may be, of another person. The Will of another person may incite and arouse the activities of one's Desire and Imagination, and render it so active that it will drag into action its own mate, the Will of the person affected. And, in the same way, a strong Desire in the mind of a person, may act to arouse into activity the Will of another, taking the latter away from its lawful mate—the Desire of the person affected. In the same way, two Wills (that of the person affected and that of the person affecting) may struggle for the control, mastery and possession of the Desire and Imagination of the first mentioned person. And, likewise, there is often found the struggle between the feminine principle of Desire in two persons, each wishing to maintain and exert influence over the Will of one of the persons. In this statement is contained the actual secret of the Mental Influence of one person over another in direct personal relations and contact. It is the secret underlying hypnotism, mental influence, personal magnetism, psychic influence, and all the other forms of direct mental influence.

The same principle is operative in the case of mental influence at a distance. In it is found the explanation of the Law of Attraction; the Drawing Power of the Mind; Absent Treatments; etc., as well as in the various forms of phenomena generally grouped together under the head of Mental Magic. There is found the effect of the masculine Will principle in the thought-waves and mental currents upon the feminine principle of Desire in the minds of those affected. And likewise there is found the attractive force of the strong feminine Desire thought-waves or mental currents, which tend to attract and arouse into activity the masculine principle or Will of those affected. *It should be unnecessary to state that every person, male or female, has this dual-principle of mind within him or her—the masculine and the feminine mental phases of mind.*

The feminine principle of mind acts always in the direction of exerting an attracting, drawing influence upon the will; and also in the direction of creating and conceiving ideas, mental images and other forms of mental creative activity. The masculine principle of mind always acts in the direction of inciting activity within the feminine principles of mind. The feminine principles of mind may be said to be dominated and ruled by the masculine principle, so far as the apparent workings of the mind is concerned; but as a matter of fact, a closer examination will disclose the interesting fact that the masculine principle is always attracted and *"managed"* by the feminine principle, either its own lawful mate, or else the feminine principle of some other mind. We have seen in a preceding lesson, that the Will is "free" and theoretically at least may act without restraint from within, but that in reality it never *does* act unless aroused by Desire. It can "act as it *pleases,*" but the "pleases" depends upon Desire, the feminine principle. So that in mental phenomena, as in human life, while the masculine is apparently, and theoretically, the master, as a matter of fact, the feminine causes her mate to do as *she* "pleases," at the same time allowing him to think that it is *he* who "pleases."

The men and women of strong Will Power, who dominate all around them, and often those far removed from them in space, really emanate strong currents charged with Will Power, which coming in contact with the feminine principles in the minds of others arouse the latter and cause the desires of those persons to be in accord with the Will of the strong individual. Great masters of men possess this power to a great degree, and then "work their Will" upon others in this way. Their influence is felt far and near, and they make people do as they like by making them "want to" do that way, or else by causing them to "fear," which is but a negative form of Desire, as we have said in another lesson. In the same way, men of strong Desire and Imagination—feminine principles of the mind—may and do exert powerful influence over the minds and Wills of others, and lead them their way. The "magnetic" persons manifest these feminine principles—they attract, allure, draw on, and often actually seduce the Wills of other people. They are emotional, and capture the Will of others, and at the same time produce a consequent reaction on the emotional natures of the others, by sympathetic vibration. The "electric" persons manifest the masculine principle and cause others to "want to" do as the person wishes. They are "motional" and not only arouse the Desire in others, but also overawe and terrorize the Will of the others. The men and women of the greatest power are those who manifest both the masculine and the feminine principles and consequently affect others on the lines of both poles of their mentality. One moment they exert the power of Will; the next the attracting, drawing, charming power of Desire. If you will test all instances and classes of the phenomena of Mentalism by this principle of Mental Sex Polarity, you will see that it affords an explanation and a reason for them all. We shall have more to say on this subject in our supplementary book, "The Mystery of Sex; or, Sex Polarity," of which general subject it forms a phase and part. The principle of Sex is strongly in evidence on the mental plane—as it is on the physical—and as it also is on the spiritual. He who leaves Sex Polarity out of the consideration loses the Master Key to the Creative Activities of the Cosmos. It lies indeed at the very heart of the cosmos itself.

So much for the influence of mind over mind. What of the influence of Mind over Things? The answer to this question is very simple. There *is mind in everything,* to respond to the more positive mind. Moreover, *everything is in mind*—in the Cosmic Brain. As we have said elsewhere: If Thoughts become Things in the Cosmic Brain, then following the Law of Analogy, it is possible for Thoughts to materialize as Things on other planes of activity. The same principle is involved—the principle of mental creative activity.... With a Cosmos, *mental in its nature,* with energy and substance; matter and motion; all receptive, responsive, and plastic, and obedient to Mind—what cannot be accomplished by those who understand the Laws of Mentalism? With Will as the great creative Power in the Cosmos—what is not possible to him who understands the Art of Willing? With Desire as the great creative energy, can we not see why Desire should be harnessed, controlled, directed, mastered and employed in our lives, careers and destinies?

The Arcane Teaching

LESSON XVIII.

INVOCATION AND EVOCATION.

Under the head of "Invocation and Evocation" we shall group that general class of occult phenomena which consists of the "calling upon" supernatural beings; or the "calling forth" of disembodied entities; elementals; vitalized thought entities; etc., from the Astral Plane of Existence. The word "invoke" means "To call for solemnly, or with earnestness; to call upon or address in prayer; to solicit in prayer for assistance or protection." The word "evoke" means: "To call out or summon forth; often used in the sense of calling forth of the disembodied souls, and similar entities."

Invocation of the power of superior, or supernatural beings, by means of prayer, offerings, sacrifices, and other ceremonial forms is seemingly as old as the race. All the ancient peoples invoked their greater and lesser deities, and other supernatural beings, and down to the present time we find prayer actively employed in all forms of religious worship. Even outside of the field of religion, we find many instances of invocation of the power of genii and other supernatural beings, by means of ceremonial magic and similar practices. The old works upon the Magic Art are filled with directions for ceremonials of this kind. The modern mind, however, regards these latter things as merely the effects of silly credulity on the part of ignorant people, the prejudice generally extending to the religious practice of invoking the power of the angels, saints, and other superior disembodied entities.

But, even the most ardent objector to the invocation of lesser beings, if he remain in the bosom of the churches, is apt to adhere to the old and well established custom of calling upon Deity for assistance in the affairs of his life, often going so far as to offer to Deity supposedly valuable hints and bits of advice regarding the conduct, operation and management of the Universe at large. To a mind which has grasped the realization of the transcendent ideal of the Absolute and the Infinite, it is startling to hear many devout "class-leaders," deacons and clergymen, particularly among certain non-ritualistic denominations, addressing their Deity in terms of easy familiarity and good-fellowship, giving Him their opinion on things in general; finding fault; administering patronizing commendation and flattery; and in general informing Him how they, the invokers, wish the world to be managed and run. Burns's poem, "Holy Willie's Prayer" gives us an excellent example of this form. This, however, is a statement of an extreme abuse of the principle, and our natural revolt at the same must not blind us to the fact that prayer in other forms constitutes a source of great spiritual comfort and consolation to many a soul in hours of trouble and pain.

The modern rationalist, seeing no intellectual "reason" for believing in the efficacy of prayer, is apt to dismiss the entire subject as but a part of the outgrown superstition of the race. But this will not do, for an unprejudiced observer will find before him many striking and undoubted instances of "answer to prayer"—of results occurring in almost exact accordance with the nature of earnest and sincere invocation. These instances are too numerous and common to be dismissed as mere coincidence—they must be admitted, and the cause looked for further. And in the examination and search, we must not lose sight of the too often overlooked fact, that these "answers to prayer" come to people of all shades of heterodox religious belief—heathen, pagan, idolators, in all parts of the globe, and in all times—as well as to "true believers" in the particular faith which happens to be "orthodox" in our particular land at this particular time. The worshippers of the ancient gods of Rome and Greece had their prayers answered; the Egyptian worshippers had the same favors granted them; the Hindus, ancient and modern, received great benefits from prayer; the Mohammedans are a people of great prayers, and many are the answers received by the faithful Moslem. And so, the investigator must either accept the polytheistic idea of the existence of many gods of many people, all of whom hear and answer the prayers of their worshippers, or else the alternative idea that all of these various worshippers, while worshipping at their respective shrines and altars, in reality bring themselves in psychic communication with higher spiritual powers, and thus set in operation natural psychic forces which tend to bring to them their "heart's desire." Which of the two ideas seem the most rational and in accordance with the known facts of the universe?

The Arcane Teachers have always held and taught that every true and earnest prayer coming from the heart of a sincere and devout worshipper, tends to bring that person into a closer relation to the great Cosmic Spirit—the Essence of the One Life of the Cosmos. This, not by a reaching out of the person's mind toward some far away Something, but by means of an Inward Unfoldment, by which the Spirit within each soul unfolds itself and is recognized as present and existent. This experience of the Indwelling Presence of Deity, or the Union with Deity, is common to the religiously inclined soul of all lands, times, and phases of belief—it is common to the race. Instances are found in the records of the transcendental of all times.

This experience, when it occurs to one, leaves him with a sense of renewed power and strength, which often operates in the direction of the person being able to accomplish that for which he prayed. Not only does it act as a Comforter, but also as a Source of Power. And this is not to be wondered at, when we realize that it means that the individual is thus brought much closer to the very Essence of Being—the One Life. An understanding of this fact will enable us to understand many instances of renewed strength resulting from prayer, meditation, and self-communion, which cannot be dismissed lightly as "mere imagination." All advanced occultists realize the benefits which result from "Meditation," in which the same principle is invoked. When one comes into close relationship with the Cosmic Will, is it any wonder that Power results?

But there is more to the subject than even this. The person who prays earnestly and with *faith in the result,* assumes the mental attitude of Confident Expectation, which is one of the first stages in Attainment by occult methods. Earnest Demand; Confident Expectation; Positive Will—these are the three Co-ordinates of the exercise of Occult Power. And the first two elements are present in all earnest, faithful prayer. And the final stage is very often awakened by the exercise of the two former. More over, in demanding earnestly, and expecting faithfully, the person creates the mental image in the Imagination which is an important part in all manifestation of occult power. By exerting these mental forces, all of them important and effective, is it any wonder that the person sets into operation the mental forces which tend to draw to him the things that he needs—and to materialize the ideals that he is holding in his mind? It would be a source of wonder to all occultists if the said results failed to manifest in some degree. The laws of Mentalism are set into full operation by earnest, heartfelt, faithful prayer—it is one of the most potent forms of invoking the operation of well established laws of Mentalism. This is apparent to all advanced occultists—and will be to the student, if he will but analyze the processes and methods employed unconsciously by the devout worshipper.

And, moreover, none of us can afford to sneer at the tales of the interposition of "the saints" and "angels," and other "holy beings" of the several religions. These are no mere fantasies, and vain imaginings. While many of the beneficent results attributed to them are really due to the causes above mentioned, still all occultists know that there are many advanced beings on the higher planes of the Cosmos, who are undoubtedly attracted by persons on the lower planes who bring themselves in *rapport* with them by manifesting the proper mental and spiritual states. "There are many more things in heaven and on earth" than are dreamt of in the philosophies of the day. But, of course, any and all results of prayer are in full accord with natural law, and result through the operations thereof. These things are not supernatural—they are but a part of Nature's hidden workings.

Let us now consider the subject of "Evocation."

One of the most common of all forms of Evocation is the familiar "materialization" of disembodied human beings by means of a "medium," or person in the flesh, whose vital power is used by the disembodied entity in manifesting itself once more on the material plane. In some of the instances of this form of manifestation the disembodied entity voluntarily and consciously makes use of the vitality of the medium in order to manifest itself to persons in the flesh for the purpose of communicating with them, or else merely to gratify a desire to assume earthly form and garb once more, and to mingle with persons in the flesh. But all true occultists are aware that a large percentage of these manifestations are not the entities which they purport to represent, but are imposters from the Astral Plane, who assume the image of friends and relatives of those present, copying with more or less perfect detail the mental image of the departed one which exists in the mind of the person in the flesh, and which is called forth by memory by the associations and suggestions of the *seance*.

Another form of Evocation, also quite common in *seances,* is that where the disembodied entity is actually "called forth" by the strong desire and affection of some of the visitors attending the seance, in which case the materialization is effected through the vital powers of the medium, inspired into activity by the strong desire of those who wish to communicate with and see once more the form of those who have passed out of the flesh. In these cases the disembodied entity is scarcely conscious of the manifestation, and is like a person in a dream, or rather like one who walks in his sleep. This fact accounts for the dazed, startled condition of mind often manifested by these materialized entities when they are summoned forth at a *seance*. They are dwelling in the life of the Astral Plane, wrapt in their owns dreams and meditations, and it is cruel to disturb them. In fact, it is quite as unnatural to place a disembodied entity in this condition as it is to plunge a person in the flesh into some abnormal psychic state. Advanced occultists, unanimously, condemn the prevalent practice of evoking these entities, and disturbing their Astral life.

There is a class of earth-bound entities on the lowest sub-planes of the Astral Plane, who hover around their old scenes on earth so long as they are allowed to do so by the laws of the Astral World. These entities swarm around materialization seances, and other similar psychic performances, taking great delight in manifesting their presence as forcibly as may be, and playing as many pranks as possible. These entities often act the part of some celebrated character of history, or some friend or relative of those present, and make "exhibitions" of themselves by making Shakespeare write doggerel verse; or Napoleon tell someone what to take to get rid of a cold; or Plato to warn a maiden to "beware of the 'light-complected' woman." This fact has brought genuine spiritualistic phenomena into disrepute in many quarters where the state of affairs is not known, and caused much pain and heart-burnings among the sincere early followers of spiritualism who were not acquainted with these psychic facts, but who accepted as "gospel truth" every communication reaching them from the "spirit world."

The average spiritualist of to-day, however, is much better informed, and is disposed to be quite as particular in forming "spirit" acquaintances and friendships, as he is in forming earthly ones. Much of the testimony given at *seances* by even reputable and truthful entities is more or less incorrect for reasons that will be apparent to those who have read what we said in our lesson on the "Astral Plane." That is to say, these entities, as a rule, are familiar only with the particular environment familiar to them by reason of their affiliations and their particular character. The best proof of this is the totally contradictory evidence offered by such entities. Their reports range all the way from the "happy hunting grounds" of the savage, to the state of transcendental bliss of the idealistic soul. And each of these reports are equally true, for each reports "the Thing as he sees it," for the world "of Things as they are" on the Astral Plane. When these facts are understood, one may begin to reconcile the apparent discrepancies of the reports of the *seance*.

In some cases disembodied entities may fall in with the desires of those in the flesh, and will endeavor to aid them in their purposes in the earth-life. But they can accomplish no more than if "they were in the flesh—they can employ the thought-force in the same manner—that is all. They cannot affect a person whose thoughts are of a higher degree of vibration, any more than can be done by one still in the flesh. The influence of these entities has been grossly exaggerated by some writers on the subject. They are governed by the Law of Attraction, and can go only where they are attracted. Moreover, they are apt to end in tormenting those who have invoked them for unworthy purposes. We caution all against attempting to make use of such aid, even if offered.

There is also the Evocation of what are called in a general way, "the elementaries" or "elemental forces." We do not consider it wise to enter into a detailed consideration of this subject, for reasons which will be apparent to all advanced students of occultism. We have spoken of it in a previous lesson. Enough to say that in nature there are semi-intelligent living forces, which under certain conditions may be evoked and guided by the intelligence of human beings, in certain forms of Black Magic. Such practices are extremely unworthy, and invariably result in disastrous results to those dabbling in the forbidden practices. We assure the student, however, that these influences can work no harm to those who stand on the higher plane of thought and life, although those on the lower planes of thought and life may suffer annoyance from them. The Law of Attraction governs and regulates these things—"like attracts like"; "entities, like water seek always their own level."

Another form of Evocation, very common and yet scarcely recognized by many thinkers along these lines, is the evocation of Thought Forms, Desire Nebulae, etc. These peculiar Things are the result of strong and vital currents of Will and Desire thrown off from the minds of persons who have lived, and who may still be living. They have a tendency to coalesce and combine, and following the Law of Attraction they gather in the vicinity where similar mental influences are being exerted. They are like gathering clouds on the horizon, non active in themselves, but capable of manifesting lightning and thunder under certain conditions. These lacking conditions are often supplied by persons of strong Desire or Will, who attract them to them and vitalize them by the energy of their own emotions or motive mentality. These thought-clouds then act as if they had been sent out by the mind of the person animating and energizing them, and manifest all the phenomena of the thought currents. They may either be directed toward the accomplishment of certain ends of the person, if he be capable of such direction; or, on the contrary, they may involve him in a psychic whirlwind or tempest until he is almost torn asunder. The consequence is that one often "sows the wind, and reaps the whirlwind" is literal truth. Beginning with manifesting these mental states, one is finally carried off his mental feet by them, and caused great pain and misfortune. The lives of many prominent men show examples of this phenomena, although the public does not understand it.

Akin to the above, is the evocation of the Desire Elementals, and "artificial entities" mentioned in our lesson "The Astral Plane." In this case the effect is even more startling than that arising from the evocation of Thought Forms, etc., to which the Desire Elementals are closely related. The difference between the Desire Elementals and active Thought Forms is only a matter of degree, and many writers confuse the two forms of manifestation.

It should be unnecessary for us to add that the Arcane Teachers most positively condemn the practice of evoking the elementals, and forbid it among their students. In fact, they withhold the inner teachings on the subject of certain sub-planes of the Astral, as we have seen, in order to prevent unworthy persons taking advantage of certain of the Teachings. The practice of Evocation often leads directly to Black Magic, which involves the practitioner in whirlwinds and whirlpools of psychic energy and occult forces, and often causes his destruction. There are many to-day practicing Evocation, under high sounding names, and clothed with the garments of high pretensions. But such will feel the Law of Cause and Effect. The Law is never mocked. It moves with the pitiless and unerring certainty of a machine. Each draws his own to him. None can escape their own good—or evil. Beware of Evocations! Do not play with fire. Do not toy with Edged Tools!

PART VII. ARCANE SECRETS.

Lesson XIX. The Secret of The Opposites.

Lesson XX. The Secret of Rhythm.

Lesson XXI. The Secret of Balance.

LESSON XIX.
THE SECRET OF THE OPPOSITES.

Let us now consider The Law of Opposites, or Polarity, the mastering of which constitute one of the Arcane Secrets. Listen to the Aphorism:
Aphorism XXI Every thing in the Cosmos has its opposite. Every quality, attribute or condition has its opposite. Every thing and every quality, attribute or condition is one of a Pair of Opposites—and yet contains within itself a Pair of Opposites. Polarity is inherent in every thing. Every thing has its Two Poles; and also is, itself, one pole of something else. The Pairs of Opposites—the two Opposing Poles—are but phases of the same thing. In the union of the Two Poles, or Pair of Opposites, there is to be found the "thing-in-itself" of a thing. There is always a Reconciliation and Agreement possible between Opposites—always a possible Synthesis of Opposing Thesis and Antithesis. Every thing "is" and "is not" at the same time, in its qualities, attributes and conditions—and the Reconciliation, Agreement and Synthesis reveals a new "Is." And yet the Reconciliation, Agreement, or Synthesis—the new "Is"—is but one Pole, or one of a Pair of Opposites, of a new and higher Polarity or Pair. And, so on, to infinity. In this Aphorism is contained the Secret of the Understanding of all things in the Cosmos.

This Aphorism states a fundamental truth of the Arcane Teaching—the truth that everything is but one pole of a Pair of Opposites. And that while every thing has its Opposite, still the two Opposites, together, form the Real Thing. Every truth is but a half truth. Everything is a paradox. There is "the other side" to everything. There are the "two extremes" to every thing. In this great Cosmic Law is found the fact that diametrically opposed things, physical, mental and spiritual, are in reality but the different poles of the same thing. In this Law is found the explanation of all physical phenomena—the mental activities and states—and the Secret of Sex—Generation and Regeneration—and many other important facts and laws of Cosmic Activity.

When one has had his attention directed to the existence of The Law of Opposites, he will see evidences of its presence and operation on all sides, and in all phenomena of the Cosmos. He will soon see that no matter what may be the quality of a thing, another quality diametrically opposed to the first one will always be found. Sometimes it is difficult to discover the opposing quality—but the Law is invariable and constant, and a careful search will always reveal the Opposite.

The principle may be called to your mind by reference to a few familiar instances. Thus: You will always find an Up and a Down; a High and a Low; a Right and a Left; a Hard and a Soft; a Heavy and a Light; an Abstract and a Concrete; a Long and a Short; a Broad and a Narrow; a Hot and a Cold; a Sharp and a Dull; an Easy and a Difficult; a North and a South; an East and a West; a Positive and a Negative; a Male and a Female; a Large and a Small; a Good and a Bad; a Light and a Dark; a Day and a Night; a Love and a Hate; a Courage and a Fear; a Truth and an Untruth; and so on until you will find that, the moment you notice a quality of a thing, that same moment you will recognize an opposite quality.

Your first impression after noticing these Pairs of Opposites is that they are composed of things entirely different from each other—entirely apart—and far from being "the same thing." But examine a little closer, and what do you see? Where do you draw the line between Up and Down? You may say that one thing is "up" and another "down," in comparison with each other, or in relation to some other thing. But, in the abstract, apart from comparison and relativity—where is your dividing line which causes one direction in Space to be "up" and another to be "down." You will find that there is no such absolute division, and that your "up" and "down" are but relative and comparative terms, depending upon some imaginary or temporary dividing line.

Astronomers recognize this fact, and one of the first things they teach their students is: "There is no 'up' nor 'down' in Space!" The same is of course true with High and Low; Right and Left; etc. Also with the cardinal points, which consist of Pairs of Opposites. Travel North as far as you can go, and reaching the North Pole you find yourself in a position in which whatever direction you travel your next step will lead you South. Travel East as far as you can and you will find yourself returning to your starting point *from the West*—for there is no "East or West Pole." What is West to us, is East to others. China and India are in the "Great East," but they are

West to America. We can reach them by travelling either East or West.

You think that Hard and Soft are two entirely different things, do you not? Then tell us where you draw the line between Hard and Soft. What constitutes a thing Hard or Soft—except relativity and comparison? Where is your Absolute Hard, or Absolute Soft? Hard and Soft are but names for *degrees* of a Something the two Opposites or Poles of which we call "Hard" and "Soft," respectively. The same is true of Heavy and Light. Where is your dividing line? The terms are but *relative degrees* of weight, are they not?—poles of the same thing. What is the difference between Long and Short—Broad and Narrow—Sharp and Dull? These contrasting qualities are but *degrees* in the same thing. What is the difference between Large and Small? What particular size makes one thing Large and another Small? Where is your standard? What is the difference between an Easy thing and a Difficult one? Is there a positive standard—are they not merely *degrees* of the same thing, and relative to the strength of power employed?

Perhaps this point can be brought out more clearly by a consideration of "Hot and Cold." At first thought no two things seem further removed from one another than these two—they seem to have nothing in common. But let us see. We find that science assumes the existence of a certain Something called "Temperature." The word is derived from a Latin Word Meaning "measure; proportion; degree." Science uses it to indicate the "intensity of radiant heat." And Heat is held to be simply a "state or condition of matter, resulting from vibration." Temperature then is merely a term used to indicate *varying degrees of vibration* of a certain kind. Therefore we see that "Hot and Cold" have no real existence as things-in-themselves, but are merely *degrees* in the scale of Heat, the latter being but a term indicating certain kinds of vibrations. Therefore "Hot and Cold" are but degrees of the same thing, in the end—and that "same thing" is but a quality of Something Else—a quality of Motion, having its own Opposite in a higher scale.

Moreover, even on the lower plane "Hot and Cold" are seen to be but relative and comparative. At what point on the thermometer would you draw a line dividing "Hot" from "Cold"? Everything is a little "hotter" than something else, and a little "colder" than a third thing. So far as the sensation of "Hot" and "Cold" is concerned, it is quite relative and comparative. Come from a cold hallway, into a warmer room, and you feel quite warm, even though those in the room be shivering. Dip one hand into ice-water, and the other into boiling water, at the same time—and then plunge both hands into a basin of luke-warm water, at the same moment. What is the result? To one hand the water seems quite warm, while to the other it seems quite cool—and yet the temperature of the water is fixed. Where is your "Hot and Cold," then? You say that to-day is "warm" meaning that it is warmer than it has been. A month from now, you may call the same temperature "cool." In the end you will find that "Hot and Cold" are but names designating *degrees* of Heat vibration. You know very well what you mean by each term—you recognize them as Opposites—and yet you are unable to fix a dividing line between them or to separate things into two distinct classes of "Hot" and "Cold" respectively. You find that they blend into each other, and that the shades of differences between close degrees are almost indistinguishable in sensation. You see that they are but a Pair of Opposites, and together form Two Poles of the same thing—Heat. The very "Cold" thing is as much *a degree of Heat* as is the very "Hot" thing—the distinction is merely one of *degree.*

The same Law is operative in the field of Good and Bad. (We do not refer to "Right and Wrong" in the moral or religious sense, although even that comes under the Law, and is a matter of *degrees* upon a standard erected by some particular school, religion, or custom—the standard varying greatly among the schools, sects, or localities. It is often very difficult to determine between "Right and Wrong" in any particular standard or scale, so closely do the degrees shade into each other.) We refer to "Good" in the sense of: "desirable; conducive to satisfaction and happiness"; and to "Bad" in the sense of: "undesirable; conducive to dissatisfaction and unhappiness." We find, upon analysis and examination, that these two terms are but another Pair of Opposites, which represent degrees of a Something which we may call "Satisfaction" or "Happiness." A "Good" thing is one which causes Happiness and Satisfaction; a "Bad" thing, one which produces Unhappiness and Dissatisfaction. We readily distinguish between these two results, in general. But when it comes to drawing a fixed line between them on the scale, we find it impossible. Some things are "better" than others; some things are "worse" than others; but these degrees are comparative, and relative. A dirty crust of dry bread tastes very "good" to a starving man; while the same thing would be very "bad" to the taste of a well fed person. And so it is with everything "Good and Bad"—all relative.

Moreover, the same thing may be both "Good and Bad," at the same time—that is, "Good" for some purposes and "Bad" for others. So we must always inquire "Good" for *what?* "Bad" for *what?* And, likewise, the same thing may be both "Good and Bad," at the same time, for the same purpose, *for two different people.* "It's an ill wind that blows Nobody any Good," says the proverb. "One man's Good is another man's Bad," says another. "One man's Loss is another man's Gain," says a third. "One man's Meat is another man's Poison," says a fourth. And so on, each illustrating the truth of the general statement. A "Good day's fishing" may be a "Bad day's work" for the fish. "Good!" says one man when wheat advances on the Board of Trade—and yet that advance may mean the greatest "Bad" for another. A writer on Natural History once pointed to the long legs and long beak of the Crane, so well adapted to catching fish, as a "mark of the Goodness of Providence." The fish probably thought it an exceedingly "Bad" provision.

Let us begin with the Positive Pole of Love-Hate, which we call "Love." We find here a high degree of the emotional quality which consists of the states of "affection; regard; attraction; affinity; etc." Then, on the extreme Opposite of the scale—the Negative Pole—we find the quality which we call "Hate," which consists of "aversion; dislike; repulsion; etc." These two emotional states seem as different as any two things can be, do they not? It seems almost impossible to conceive that they are but the Opposite Poles of what we may call "Regard" or "Attraction," or "Affinity"—and yet such is their real relation. Returning once more to the pole of "Love," let us descend the scale. Moving down a little on the scale we find states of "less regard," or "less attraction." Then still further down, we find states in which the regard or attraction is very greatly reduced. Finally we come to a point at which there appears to be *no* regard or attraction, and still *no* repulsion or dislike. This is the neutral point of balance which is always to be found somewhere in the consideration of every Pair of Opposites, and yet which is not a fixed or absolute point, but which varies according to circumstances, persons and various influences. Then passing down the scale we find manifested a slight repulsion or dislike; this increases as we move down the scale. Finally we notice degrees of intense dislike and repulsion, until finally we find the Negative Pole of "Hate." You will understand this readily—you have noticed the different degrees of Love and Hate, and have also noticed how these degrees rise and fall according to circumstances and conditions. But have you ever noticed that extreme Love often is suddenly transmuted into extreme Hate, and *vice versa,* under extreme emotion or exciting cause. Who has not seen instances where a woman's intense Love has been transformed into burning Hate, by the influence of some new cause. In some cases the emotion moves rapidly backward and forward, to-and-fro, between these two poles, until the person does not know whether he or she Loves or Hates. As in one of Kipling's poems a woman says: "I 'ate you, grinnin' there. . . . Ah, Gawd, I *love* you so!"

It will be seen that all these transmutations of emotional states from one pole to the other—from Love to Hate—from Fear to Courage—are but changes of Polarity, or a shifting of position on the emotional scale. But these changes are *always* along the scale of the emotion which has the two poles—and not from one emotion to another. Emotions of different scales cannot be transmuted one to another—they must belong to the same scale. Water may be transformed into Steam, and Wood into Smoke; but Water cannot be transformed into Smoke, nor Wood into Steam. And so it is with the emotional states—*the transmutation must be along the degrees of, or between the poles of, the same scale.*

And, so, now we arrive at the point of the Arcane Teaching in which is made plain the processes of Mental Transmutation in its phase of Change of Polarity. This forms an important part of the Arcane Processes of Mental Transmutation. By the application of the trained Will, it is possible for the student to *transmute one emotional state to its opposite,* by changing the polarity. Thus, one may change his Love into Hate, or his Hate into Love, simply by concentrating the Attention and Will upon the Opposite Pole of the state or quality. In the Arcane processes, the student is never told to "fight" or "kill out" an undesirable emotional quality by opposing sheer Will to it—this is a waste of energy, and is moreover quite unscientific. The proper method is *to concentrate on the Opposite Pole,* and thus change the vibrations and shift the emotional center of Balance.

In the same way, and under the same Law, the emotional states of others may be influenced by polarizing their minds on the opposite pole of the scale of the emotion in question. Hate is not to be combatted by Hate—this only adds fuel to the fire. The proper way is to form the mental image of Like and Attraction, in your mind, and then concentrate its effects upon the other person. Just as you may change your own emotional states, so may you change his, under the proper conditions and by the proper methods. And, remember this, this process does not consist in the sentimental, negative, rabbit-like attitude of mind that many teachers preach to the students—it does not consist in "turning the other cheek" to be smitten. Far from it, this process is purely volitional and not emotional. It is the bringing into play of the scientific principles of Mentalism—not wishy-washy emotional sentimentalism, or the practice of "kissing the rod that smites you." The Arcanes are not sentimentalists, nor emotional weaklings. On the contrary, *they live in their heads* with their Balance in the Will. But, nevertheless, they tell you that the way to combat Hate is by its opposite Pole. This is a Paradox which requires thought to solve. It is the principle taught in the old fable, in which the Sun and the North Wind dispute their power to tear away a man's cloak from him. The harder the North Wind blew, the closer the man hugged the cloak around him. But when the Sun tried the effect of its heated rays, the man soon dropped the cloak because he found it uncomfortable. Polarizing in an Opposite, negates the first condition.

If you are strong enough to hear the full truth, listen to these words: The advanced occultist regards *both* Love and Hate as emotions of the "Me" side of oneself. Therefore he rises above both, and neither Loves nor Hates, in the ordinary meaning of the terms. He maintains a balance in his "I," like the man on the tight rope with his balancing pole, first shifting the balance to one side, and then to the other, as occasion renders advisable. He thinks that the slave to Love is as miserable as the slave to Hate—and he avoids both extremes. He finds that the synthesized Love-Hate is in itself but one pole of a Something Else—and he moves up higher to that Something. Instead of being compelled to sail according to the wind of Emotion, he ploughs his way through the Sea of Life by the power of the Steam of Will. He knows the Opposites—the Two Poles—of everything, to be but phases of a Synthesis of opposite qualities. He changes them to suit himself and his purposes. He solves the problem of the "two ends" *by tying them together.* He is Balanced between the Two Poles. He neutralizes unnecessary qualities, and undesirable ones, by changing their polarity. He grasps both horns of the Dilemma. He embraces the Paradox as a Whole. He claims all—but allows naught to claim him. He uses all—but allows naught to use him. Along this road lies Mastery!

The Arcane Teaching

LESSON XX.
THE SECRET OF RHYTHM.

Let us now consider the Law of Rhythm, the mastery of which constitutes one of the Arcane Secrets. Listen to the Aphorism:

APHORISM XXII. In the Cosmos every thing moves. Every thing is in constant motion. Every thing is undergoing constant change. Every thing "beats time." Vibration is universal, and, manifesting according to the Law of Rhythm, constitutes the difference of degree existing between things on all planes. Every thing moves to-and-fro in Rhythm, between its two poles. Every thing rises and falls, in Rhythm, within the limits of its nature. Every thing advances and retreats, in Rhythm, within the limits of its power.

The Aphorism informs us of the truth that in the Cosmos everything moves; is in constant motion; is undergoing constant change. This is one of the fundamental principles of the ancient instruction of the Arcane Teachers, which has been steadfastly adhered to throughout the centuries, until now the most advanced modern science has moved to the same position. Heraclitus, the famous Greek philosopher, who lived nearly twenty-five hundred years ago, and who was affiliated with the Arcane School, made this principle the basis of his philosophy. His basic principle was: "Everything moves; everything changes; everything is in flux; everything is constantly 'becoming.'" Clodd, the English scientific writer, says: "Nothing escapes the law of change. The shrewd speculations of Heraclitus, the Ionion, who lived two thousand five hundred years ago, that everything is in a state of flux, and, therefore, that the universe is always "becoming," have added confirmation in every discovery of modern physics." Buddha (B. C. 600) said: "Everything changes but Change."

Huxley said: "The more we learn of the nature of things, the more evident is it that what we call rest is only unperceived activity; that seeming peace is silent but strenuous battle. In every part, at every moment, the state of the cosmos is the expression of a transitory adjustment of contending forces; a scene of strife in which all the combatants fall in turn. What is true of each part is true of the whole. Natural knowledge tends more and more to the conclusion that 'all the choir of heaven and furniture of the earth' are transitory forms or parcels of cosmic substances wending along the road of evolution, from nebulous potentiality, through endless growths of sun and planet and satellite; through all varieties of matter; through infinite diversities of life and thought; possibly, through modes of being of which we have neither a conception, nor are competent to form any, back to the indefinable latency from which they arose. Thus the most obvious attribute of the cosmos is its impermanence."

The universal and ceaseless motion of all things is caused, of course, by the operation of the Principle of Motion—one of the Three Cosmic Principles, which acts upon Substance in the many manifestations arising principally from the action and reaction of the dual principles of, or rather the opposite poles of, Attraction-Repulsion. Its forms and varieties are as manifold as are those of Substance, or Consciousness—that is to say, they are practically infinite. The basic activity of Motion, however, is that which we call Vibration, of which the Aphorism says: "Vibration is universal, and manifesting according to the Law of Rhythm, constitutes the difference of degrees between things on all planes." Modern Science now stands "on all fours" with the Arcane Teaching in this respect, and not only holds that all things are in constant vibration, but also, that the rates of vibration determine the difference in the elemental nature of all things. Everything, from the tiny corpuscle, or electron, of which the atoms are composed, to the greatest masses of matter known to us, manifest the law of Rhythmic Vibration. Moreover, Science has demonstrated that the sole difference between the "elements" which make up the different forms of matter, arises from the rate and degree of vibration manifested by the electrons composing them—that is to say, they are *but varying degrees of vibration*. The difference between Gold and Lead consists but of differences in Vibration. The difference between Light and Beeswax is but a difference in Vibration.

In previous lessons you have seen that the Cosmos, when resolved into the Infinity of Nothingness, is practically Motionless—the Principle of Motion is in a condition of Absolute Rest, And yet, that Absolute Rest is analogous to Motion of such a high degree of Vibration as to be practically Motionless and at Rest. In this condition, or state, the two poles of Motion have been resolved into one—the extremes have merged—Absolute Motion and Absolute Rest are seen to be identical. But from the first Dawn of the new Cosmic Day, there is manifested Vibration on a constantly descending scale, until the lowest point is reached—then the upward trend begins. And in these varying degrees of Vibration is manifested every thing that is in the Cosmos, not only the physical things, but also the mental states. Every mental state, of any and all kinds, has its own degree of Vibration, which makes it what it is, and constitutes its difference from other mental states. And these mental Vibrations may be transmitted from one brain to another, in the phenomena of Mentalism.

It should not be necessary here to inform the student that that which we call sound, light, heat, magnetism, electricity, the X-Rays, and other forms of energy, are but varying forms of Vibration. And that even the most solid piece of material substance—a diamond or piece of steel, for instance, is composed of a countless number of tiny atoms, which in turn are composed of minute electrons or particles—all in constant vibratory motion, manifesting intense energy, dashing about and circling around each other, bounding and rebounding from each other, each atom resembling a solar system with its circling planets in constant motion. The elementary text-books on physical science inform their readers that every thing, and all things, of which we have any knowledge through our senses, are but appearances arising from differing rates of Vibration. And that, moreover, our only consciousness of them is the result of Vibration.

But, what of the "Law of Rhythm" which causes everything to "beat time," as the Aphorism states? Let us consider this Law, for it has a very important bearing upon Mental States and phenomena. "Rhythm," according to the accepted usage, is "movement in measured time," the most familiar instance of which is the "time" in music, which is measured by the "beats" of the metronome or the baton. And scientific investigation, as well as the ancient occult teachings, show us that *everything in the Cosmos "beats time,"* and moves in accordance with Rhythm. We see this in the swing of the planets; the beating of the human heart; the in-breathing and out-breathing of the lungs; the rise and fall of the tides; and in the operation of Vibration on every plane, in every thing. As Vibration is universal—so Rhythm is universal.

A moment's thought will show you that all the phenomena in Nature manifest this law of Rhythmic movement between two extremes. There is always the ebb-and-flow of things. Always the rhythmic swing of the pendulum between the two extremes of the thing. Day is succeeded by night; summer by winter; action by reaction; work by rest; activity by inactivity; intermittent symptoms in diseases; "good times" by "bad times" in business; exaltation, by depression. On every plane may be observed instances of this universal "pendulum swing" of Rhythm, which carries the thing to-and-from between its two polar extremes. As the Aphorism says: "Everything moves to-and-fro, in Rhythm, *between its two poles.* Everything rises and falls, in Rhythm, *within the limits of its nature.* Everything advances and retreats, in Rhythm, *within the limits of its power.*" Modern science holds that the Evolution of worlds must have had its precedent Involution, and the Evolution must be followed by Devolution—and so on, to Infinity. It holds that just as the suns and planets were evolved by stages from the nebulae, so must they return to the nebulae, in time; again to begin a new series of evolutionary world-building. Notice the quotation from Huxley, in the first part of this lesson. Herbert Spencer makes this law of Rhythm one of the principles of his philosophy.

The Arcane Teaching also shows the Law of Rhythm to be operative in the form of the Days and Nights of the Cosmos—the swing of Rhythm between the Manifest Cosmos and the Unmanifest Cosmos. The Law of Polarity, and the Law of Rhythm are twin-laws—they are bound to each other for Eternity. You will notice the resulting effect, that the rise and fall, or rhythmic pendulum swing, is determined, governed and restrained by the length of the scale of Polarity. Nothing can swing beyond the limits of its poles—nothing can exceed the limits of its nature or power. Consequently, if a thing swings far in one direction, it swings back equally far in the other. If its swing is great, its extremes are widely apart—if the swing is small, then the extremes are close together. The pendulum illustration may be applied to the phenomena on all planes. A short beat of the metronome allows the rod to move only a short distance each way—the long beat admits of a wide swing. And so, those who enjoy keenly also suffer keenly; while those whose natures allow of but limited suffering, are also capable of only a limited degree of capacity for enjoyment. A pig suffers but little, and enjoys but little; while a highly organized, sensitive, "high strung" human being, suffers the joys of heaven at times, and also the pain of hell at others. The pendulum swings as far in one direction as in the other. *Only by a Mastery of Mental Rhythm can man hope to escape the pain that his high development would otherwise bring him.*

The Arcane Teachers instruct their pupils in the Art of Mental Transmutation, by an understanding of which they may apply the energy and power of Mental Vibrations intelligently, and under the control of the Reason and the Will. When it is understood that the difference between Mental States is like the difference between the Physical Elements—merely a rate of Vibration—then Mental Transmutation or Mental Alchemy, becomes as real as the Physical Transmutation, or Physical Alchemy, of the ancients, which science is now on the eve of rediscovering. An understanding of this give one the Mastery of Self, and also the Secret of Mentalism. Moreover, an understanding of the Law of Rhythm enables one to take advantage of the flood-tide of Mental Rhythm, and a neutralizing or rising above the ebb-tide. With an understanding of the Law of Balance, one may so balance and counterbalance himself that he is not disturbed by the backward swing of the pendulum of Rhythm, but instead may take advantage of its energy and transmute it into desirable things. In this understanding comes the Poise of Power.

Let us now consider the Law of Cyclicity, which is akin to the Law of Rhythm. Listen to the Aphorism:

APHORISM XXIII. Cyclicity is akin to Rhythm, and arises by reason of it. All events tend to move in Cyclic Trend—in constant circular movement of continuous recurrence. The only escape from Cyclicity is found in the process of transmutation into Spirality. This is accomplished by Advancing the Central Point of Motion. The conversion of the Circle into the Spiral is one of the highest forms of Mental Alchemy.

The Law of Cyclicity manifests in the universal tendency of things to swing in circles. Cyclicity is an outgrowth, or more complex form, of Rhythm, The primal manifestation of Rhythm is action to-and-fro in a straight line or path—a movement backward and forward between the limits of the poles. This would be the invariable movement if the particular force manifested were the only manifestation of force or energy in that particular field of the Cosmos. But when the swinging pendulum (free to move in *any* direction) is subjected to the conflicting attractions and repulsions of other manifestations of force and energy, then is manifested the universal tendency toward the *circular* trend—the tendency to convert the straight path of the swing into a circular path or cycle. The action and reaction, the attraction and repulsion, arising from the conflict between the force of the Rhythmic swing in a straight line on the one hand, and the attractive and repellent forces from without, on the other hand, tend to swing the moving thing in a perfect circle around a Central Point of pivotal centre. And these conflicting forces are in operation through the Cosmos, and the manifestation of Cyclicity may be noticed on all planes. There is ever the evidence of the cyclic trend of things and events—the tendency to move in circles. The electrons in the atoms move in circles, just as do the planets around the sun; and just as does the sun move around some other center in space. The highest occult teachings, as well as the highest speculations of science, inform us that there is always a movement in circles around some given point; and the movement of *this* center of motion around some other center; and so on to Infinity.

The Aphorism states that: "All events tend to move in cyclic trend—in constant circular movement of continuous recurrence." And the experience of man, aided by the reports of history, bear out this statement. The student of human history is struck by the continuous cyclic trend manifested throughout the ages of history. The student of philosophy is attracted by the same evidence in his own field. And so it is with every field of human thought—Cyclic Trend is noticeable everywhere. Races and nations rise, flourish, decline and fall; only to be succeeded by others traveling over the same lines. "Westward, the star of Empire takes its flight," the center of political power constantly changing. The civilizations of Atlantis, Egypt, Chaldea, Rome and Greece arose and passed away. Our civilization is but traveling over the same general lines. All forms of political government, monarchic, autocratic, democratic, in all their variations, were known in the past as in the present. The same law is observable in the history of philosophical thought. Theories popular in Greece over two thousand years ago afterward fell into disrepute, but are now again forcing their way to the front. The scientific theories of Causation, Continuity, Determinism, and Evolution were popular in Ancient Greece over two thousand years ago. And they were likewise popular in Ancient Egypt and in India centuries before that time. Fashions in literature, dress, and manner constantly recur—traveling 'round and 'round their little circles. Laugh as we may at the absurdity of fashion in dress, nevertheless it proceeds according to Cyclic Law. Religious ideas are as old as the world—pantheism, polytheism, monotheism, and atheism—all have played their parts of fashion in religious thought, over and over again—and will play them again. The present-day revival in interest in occult thought arises from the same law.

And the life of individuals manifests the same trend and tendency. A little thought will convince you that the majority of people travel in circles in life. The same old thing over and over again, recurring at intervals of greater or lesser duration, according to the "nature" of the person. The majority of persons are like the squirrel in the cage who travels all day on his whirling wheel—but ends where he began.

"But," you may say, "if the Cosmos travels around in a continuous circle it would never progress or advance into increased consciousness." Very true! And if the individual continued in the "constant circular movement of continuous recurrence" he would never advance on The Path. The Aphorism gives us the Secret when it says: "The only escape from Cyclicity is found in the process of transmutation into Spirality. *This is accomplished by advancing the Central Point of Motion.*" If the Central Point of Motion of a Circle is moved forward, then the Circle is converted into a Spiral. The Central Point is advanced in the Cosmos by the COSMIC WILL urging forward the entire Cosmic Process, and thus converting the Cyclic Trend into a Spiral Trend—onward and upward, in advancing and rising circles toward Progress.

And by a similar process, the individual may convert the Circle of his Life Motion into an Advancing and Rising Spiral, which while carrying him around the Life Circle will at the same time raise him a stage higher at each turn. While apparently traveling around a circle, like the average person, he will be *a stage higher at each turn*. The Mountain of Attainment, around which winds the Spiral Path, is traveled only in this way. 'Round and 'round the Pilgrims travel, seemingly retracing the same steps—but in reality reaching a stage higher each circle they make. They often complain (until they learn better) saying, "I have gone 'round and 'round, and still reach nowhere." But when they compare their present stage with that of a year ago, they see that they have *advanced*. Is this not the case with you, friend? Have you not used these very words? Heed the lesson!

By advancing the Central Point, by the WILL, the wise and strong convert the Cycles into Spirals, and thus attain and advance. As the Aphorism says, this "is one of the highest forms of Mental Alchemy."

LESSON XXI.
THE SECRET OF BALANCE.

Let us now consider the Law of Balance, the mastery of which constitutes one of the Arcane Secrets. This Law may be considered in its three phases of Counterbalance, Compensation, and Poise, respectively. Let us now consider the first phase, viz., Counterbalance. Listen to the Aphorism:

APHORISM XXIV. Know ye, that in the Cosmos every thing is Counterbalanced. Every thing is set-off and offset by other things. There is always Check and Countercheck in every manifestation, on every plane, of the Cosmos.

This first phase of Balance, which is known as "Counterbalance," is a law, the operation of which is evident to every investigator of physical science. "Balance" in the Arcane usage may be defined as: "Equipoise; equilibrium; and equality of weight or force." "Counterbalance" is defined as: "Compensating balance; weight or force opposing equal weight or force." This phase of the Law of Balance, like its other phases, arises from the existence and operation of the Law of Opposites, or Polarity. Everything in the Cosmos is dual. There is always something opposed to, counterbalancing and checking something else. The Manifest Cosmos could not exist and remain operative without this law. Just as the watch or clock requires a nicely adjusted system of counterweights, countersprings, and counterbalances, in order that their opposing action may render the movement of the timepiece uniform and regular, so does the Cosmos require, and possess, an equally nicely balanced and counterbalanced system, in order that its activities may be uniform and regular.

The regular and uniform movement of the planets around the sun is made possible only through the operation of the counterbalancing forces of centrifugal and centripetal gravity, the former manifesting in the tendency of the planet to fly from the central point, the sun; and the latter manifesting in the tendency of the planet to move toward the central point, the sun. The counterbalance of these two opposing tendencies produces regular and constant movement in the elliptic orbit.

In the same way the two phases of Force or Energy oppose and counterbalance each other—one tending to build up, and the other tending to tear down. Some authorities have adopted the use of the term "Force" to designate that form of Motion which tends "to bind together two or more particles of ponderable matter, and which retards or resists motions tending to separate such particles"; for instance, Gravitation, Cohesion, Chemical Affinity, etc.

The same authorities use the term "Energy" to designate that form of Motion which tends "to separate two or more particles of ponderable matter, or of the ethereal medium, or which resists or retards the Force tending to bind them together." Clodd says: "If Force had unresisted play, all the atoms in the universe would gravitate to a common center, and ultimately form a perfect sphere in which no life would exist, and in which no work could be done. If Energy had unresisted play, the atoms in the universe would be driven asunder and remain forever separated, with the like result of changeless powerlessness. But with these two powers in conflict . . . the universe is the theatre of ceaseless redistributions of its contents."

All through living Nature is this same law of Counterbalance in force. The plant-life nourishes the animal-life, and the latter by means of its waste matter and its disintegrating forms nourishes the former. Moreover, the very *breathing* of the two great forms of life, tend to support life in each other. Animals breathe in oxygen in order to support life, and breathe out carbonic-acid gas, the latter being poisonous to animal-life. At the same time the plants, under the action of the sun's rays, break up the carbonic-acid gas, absorbing the carbon which nourishes plant-life, and releasing the oxygen needed by animal life. Thus the refuse element of the plant is the life-giving element of the animal; and the refuse element of the animal is the life-giving element of the plant. As Emerson says: "Whilst the world is thus dual, so is every one of its parts.

The entire system of things gets represented in every particle. There is somewhat that resembles the ebb and flow of the sea, day and night, man and woman, in a single needle of the pine, in a kernel of corn, in every individual of every animal tribe. There action, so grand in the elements, is repeated within these small boundaries. For example, in the animal kingdom the physiologist has observed that no creatures are favorites, but a certain compensation balances every gift and every defect."

In Nature there is always the operation of the "Check and Countercheck" mentioned in the Aphorism. Each life-form is kept in check by some other life-form. If this were not so, particular life-forms would overrun the earth. Darwin says: "There is no exception to the rule that every organic being naturally increases at so high a rate, that, if not destroyed, the earth would soon be covered by the progeny of a single pair." Clodd adds: "If all the offspring of the elephant, the slowest breeder known, survived, there would be in seven hundred and fifty years nearly nineteen million elephants alive, descended from the first pair. If the eight or nine million eggs, which the roe of a cod is said to contain, developed into adult cod-fishes, the sea would quickly become a solid mass of them. So prolific is its progeny after progeny that the common housefly is computed to produce twenty-one millions in a season; while so enormous is the laying power of the aphis, or plant-louse, that the tenth brood of one parent, without adding the products of all the generations which precede the tenth, would contain more ponderable matter than all the population of China, estimating this at five hundred million."

It is the same in plant life. If any single species were to remain unchecked, the entire globe would be covered with it inside of less than twenty years. The fungi, and other lower organisms, multiply so rapidly (some a billion-fold in an hour) that they would cover the earth in a year, if not counterchecked by nature. But the countercheck is always there. Each animal, plant or fungus has its natural enemy which preys upon it for food. *Every living thing lives upon other living things*—each according to its kind. This is one of the forms of Nature's counterchecks. This law is brought forcibly to mind when certain plants or animals are transported to other regions, without their natural enemies accompanying them, the result being that they speedily become a danger to the land, and their natural enemies have to be brought to the new region to keep them in check. Students of Evolution see in Natural Selection, and other laws of Evolution, many phases of Counterbalance and Countercheck in the Cosmos—the working out of the law that "Everything is set-off and offset by other things," as the Aphorism says. And now let us consider the second phase of the Law of Balance—the phase of Compensation—the Debit and Credit phase of the Cosmic Activities. Listen to the Aphorism.

Aphorism XXV. Know ye, that there is always a Cosmic Debit and Credit. In the Cosmos there is Absolute Compensation. The Cosmic Accounts are always evenly balanced. There is nothing furnished Free—No thing given for Nothing—in the Cosmos. The Equivalent is always demanded and rendered. The Price for Every Thing is always fixed—and Paid.

The truth embodied in the above Aphorism is recognized by the world's greatest thinkers, although the average person endeavors to deny it, and refuses to look the Truth in the face. That wonderful essay upon "Compensation" by Emerson, carries the truth to every open mind. All true philosophers have recognized the principle as in existence. Any one may see the fact, if he will stand apart and view the world-picture in the proper perspective. The idea of Compensation is based upon the phases of Counterbalance and Countercheck—upon Set-off and Offset. In short, it is always a matter of "Paying the Price." We cannot have the cake, and keep our penny, at the same time. We must always give up one thing to obtain another—we must always relinquish to attain—we must always die to live. Life is a continuous "Pay, pay, pay!" As the Aphorism informs us: "There is nothing furnished Free—No Thing given for Nothing—in the Cosmos" ; "The price for Every Thing is always fixed—and Paid." For every advantage gained, another must be surrendered. This is the Law of the Cosmos, as all wise men know it. It does one no good to deny or ignore it—it is Law, fixed, constant, immutable.

Emerson, in his essay on "Compensation," says: "The theory of the mechanic forces is another example. What we gain in power is lost in time, and the converse. The periodic or compensating errors of the planets is another instance. The influences of climate and soil in political history are another. The cold climate invigorates. The barren soil does not breed fevers, crocodiles, tigers, or scorpions. The same dualism underlies the nature and condition of man. Every excess causes a defect; every defect an excess. Every sweet has its sour; every evil its good. Every faculty which is a receiver of pleasure has an equal penalty put on its abuse. It is to answer for its moderation with its life. For every grain of wit, there is a grain of folly. For everything you have missed, you have gained something else; and for everything you gain, you lose something. If riches are increased, they are increased that use them. If the gatherer gathers too much, nature takes out of the man what she puts into his chest; swells the estate, but kills the owner. Nature hates monopolies and exceptions. The waves of the sea do not more speedily seek a lever from their loftiest tossing than the varieties of condition tend to equalize themselves. There is some leveling circumstance that puts down the overbearing, the strong, the rich, the fortunate, substantially on the same ground with all others.

Is a man too strong and fierce for society, and by temper and position a bad citizen—a morose ruffian, with a dash of the pirate in him?—nature sends him a troop of pretty sons and daughters who are getting along in the dame's classes at the village school, and love and fear for them smooths his grim scowl to courtesy. Thus she contrives to intenerate the granite and feldspar, takes the boar out and puts the lamb in, and keeps the balance true. The farmer imagines power and place are fine things. But the President has paid dear for his White House. It has commonly cost him all his peace, and the best of his manly attributes.

To preserve for so short a time so conspicuous an appearance before the world, he is content to eat dust before the real masters who stand erect behind the throne. Or do men desire the more substantial and permanent grandeur of genius? Neither has this an immunity. He who by force of will or of thought is great and overlooks thousands, has the responsibility of overlooking. With every influx of light comes new danger. Has he light? he must bear witness to the light, and always outrun that sympathy which gives him such keen satisfaction, by his fidelity to new revelations of the incessant soul. He must hate father and mother, wife and child. Has he all that the world loves and admires and covets?—he must cast behind him their admiration and afflict them by faithfulness to his truth, and become a byword and a hissing."

As we have said in a previous lesson: *The greater the capacity for joy, the greater the capacity for pain.* The swing of the pendulum of Rhythm between the two poles of the Opposites measures our relative happiness and unhappiness—comparative satisfaction or dissatisfaction. The capacity for pain is the symbol of advanced Evolution. The tramp *has* nothing and *desires* nothing beyond his immediate wants. His arc is small. Another will have much, but desires still more. His arc is large. Each, and both, fall a little short of what would constitute happiness for them. Query: which of the two is the happiest, or the most miserable?

The answer of Compensation is: "They are equal in their degree of happiness and unhappiness—in satisfaction and misery. They are twin-brothers of equal heritage."

A financial panic which makes the millionaire writhe in fear and terror, passes entirely over the tramp. The more one has, the more afraid of losing it is he; and the harder the blow if the loss occurs. Many ancient philosophical writers insisted that the measure of pain and pleasure is equally distributed between persons—although the degrees of each vary greatly. The man who makes two dollars a day and is able to save a half-dollar out of it, is possibly happier and better satisfied than he who makes a hundred and spends half as much more. What would bring happiness to a savage would bring misery to a college professor. Happiness is comparative, and so is unhappiness. We find happiness where we least expect it—and unhappiness where it surprises us. Just as "to know all, is to forgive all"; so, to know all, is to understand the relativity of satisfaction and happiness. It is said that the "back is always made strong enough to bear the burden"—we do not assert this, as a fact, but we feel *that the back gets used to the burden,* and feels it not more than other backs feel lesser burdens. And while the proverb that "God tempers the wind to the shorn lamb" may not be scientifically correct, still it is true that *the shorn lamb becomes tempered to the wind,* and "gets used to it."

Clodd says: "The simplicity of the simplest forms has been their salvation. A high organization brings with it many disadvantages, for the more complex the structure the more liable is it to get out of gear. We cannot have highly convoluted brains and at the same time digestive organs simple and renewable like those of the sea-cucumber. Death is the price paid for complexity." And pain is the natural consequence and counterbalance of complexity in life, knowledge, and possessions.

Each one has his troubles and his joys. Each his pains and his pleasures. If we knew all the inside facts concerned with others' lives we would not be willing to exchange with them, *providing we had to live exactly their same lives.* Who would wish to exchange his personal life with that of another—taking all that goes with the other's, and giving up, completely, *all* that composes his own? Each man's "cross" is fitted exactly to his particular shoulders—and each man's "crown" is adjusted nicely upon his particular brow. It takes a philosophical mind to realize this—the tendency is to consider one's own lot the very worst of all—and the other man's lot much the better. The other man is probably thinking the same about your's. *Neither would exchange, if he knew the full facts of the case*—all the counterbalances and counterchecks. Each has his own "character," *and all that goes with it.* Each has his own arc of happiness and satisfaction—with their opposite poles. As the old Egyptian proverb ran: 'What will you have?' said the gods to man. *'Take it, and pay for it!'"*

And now, let us consider the third phase of the Law of Balance—the phase of Poise. Listen to the Aphorism:

Aphorism XXVI. Poise is Power. Poise results from Balance. Balance is secured by adjusting and maintaining the Centre between the Poles of the Pairs of Opposites. By Balanced Poise the Master neutralizes Polarity and Rhythm, by resolving them into Unity. In the Heart of the Storm is Peace. In the Centre of Life there is Poise and Power. Seek it ever, O Neophyte—for in it thou shalt find thy Self.

In this Aphorism is contained the seed-thought generated in the centuries of thought and experience of the Arcane Teachers. Do not pass it by because of its simplicity. Poised Balance is the aim and goal of the Arcane Initiates. It is the Secret of Mastery. There is always a Center of Everything. But the Center exists only because of the existence of the Circumference. There is always a Point or Poise between the Poles of every Pair of Opposites. But that Point exists only because the Extremes exist. And in the Central Point is always found the Power of the Whole Event or Thing. In the Center of Gravity of the Earth, one would be able to remain in a position of Perfect Poise, unsupported except by the Concentrated Gravity of the Whole Earth. So nicely Poised that a mere effort of the Will would exert sufficient energy to propel him in any desired direction. The Power of the Opposites are concentrated at the Central Point. There is all Power to be found—and *there* only. The axiom: "Action and Reaction are Equal" indicates a Central Point in which exists the True Lever which will move the Whole. At the Center one is enabled to *use* Action and Reaction without being subject to either. The Arcane Initiate strives to attain this state of Equilibrium and Absolute Poise. He yearns to master the art of traversing the Razor edge Wire of Life, balancing himself perfectly, like the trained mental athlete that he is, by the Balancing Pole of the Opposites which he has firmly grasped. Pitting the Opposites against each other—neutralizing Pole by Pole—balancing Law by Law—the Master traverses the slender thread which separates the World of Desire from the World of Will.

Oh, Neophyte, in the Center of Life shalt thou indeed find Poise and Power. In the Heart of the Storm shalt thou find Peace. In the Center of the Cosmos shalt thou find THYSELF. He who finds the Center of Himself, finds the Center of the Cosmos. For, at the last, they are ONE.

VALE!

FINIS.

William Walker Atkinson

www.ingramcontent.com/pod-product-compliance
Lightning Source LLC
Chambersburg PA
CBHW061432040426
42450CB00007B/1023